Michelangelo Buonarroti (1475–1564) paints Prophet
Zaccariah section of the Sistine Chapel, Vatican Palace, Rome,
starting in 1508.

THE ILLUSTRATED TIMELINE OF
Religion

THE ILLUSTRATED TIMELINE OF
Religion

A CRASH COURSE IN WORDS & PICTURES

Laura S. Smith

STERLING

New York / London
www.sterlingpublishing.com

A JOHN BOSWELL ASSOCIATES BOOK

STERLING and the distinctive Sterling logo are registered trademarks of the Sterling Publishing Co., Inc.

Library of Congress Cataloging-in-Publication Data Available

2 4 6 8 10 9 7 5 3 1

Published by Sterling Publishing Co., Inc.
387 Park Avenue South, New York, NY 10016
© 2007 by Sterling Publishing, Co., Inc.
Distributed in Canada by Sterling Publishing
c/o Canadian Manda Group, 165 Dufferin Street
Toronto, Ontario, Canada M6K 3H6
Distributed in the United Kingdom by GMC Distribution Services
Castle Place, 166 High Street, Lewes, East Sussex, England BN7 1XU
Distributed in Australia by Capricorn Link (Australia) Pty. Ltd.
P.O. Box 704, Windsor, NSW 2756, Australia

Sterling ISBN-13: 978-1-4027-3606-3
ISBN-10:1-4027-3606-1

For information about custom editions, special sales, premium and
corporate purchases, please contact Sterling Special Sales
Department at 800-805-5489 or specialsales@sterlingpub.com.

Book Design by Barbara Aronica-Buck

Contents

Acknowledgments

Special thanks go to John Boswell, Christa Bourg, Kathryn Baxter, and Lauren Galit who conceived of this project and lent their expertise to make it a reality. Thanks also to our wonderful designer, Barbara Aronica-Buck, and to the team at Sterling for their impeccable fact-checking, copyediting, and other expertise.

Gratitude to my family, and my family of friends, for your unfailing support and inspiration, and for listening to me talk.

Finally, deepest thanks to my many teachers in all traditions, my students, and "all my relations." This book is for you.

May all beings be happy!

Introduction

Does religion still matter in our modern world? Or has it been rendered obsolete by the ever-accelerating pace of social and technological change that seems to increasingly demand our attention and monopolize our time?

As the following pages will show, religion and spirituality are as vital a key to understanding our times as ever. God (in the multitude of forms in which he/she/it has been portrayed, including as nothing) is not dead, as the philosopher Friedrich Nietzsche famously suggested. One has only to open today's newspaper to see that religion is alive and well and at the root of many of our most confounding problems, including warfare, acts of terrorism and the "culture wars" that increasingly dominate political life in America. Indeed, many of the defining political and cultural events throughout history had religious dimensions, often as their explicit driving force. Examples come readily to mind: the Crusades, the Protestant Reformation, and World War II to name just a few.

What is religion? It's a tricky question and scholars have put forth a wide range of definitions emphasizing a variety of approaches and disciplines. The word itself is derived from the Latin "religio" (to bind) emphasizing ritual observance. A useful working definition for understanding religion cross-culturally has been proposed by scholar Ninian Smart, which suggests that religion is that which contains the following six dimensions: Mythical, Ritual, Doctrinal, Ethical, Institutional, and Experiential. Most religions and spiritual traditions can be said to have some version of these aspects, and this framework can help us think about what defines the nature of religion from a comparative perspective.

Religious and spiritual traditions address moral and existential questions universal to human experience, questions like: What happens to us after we die? What is the nature of evil? Why do bad things happen to good people? How did the world begin? Like literature or art, religion is a universal expression of human culture that stems from the deepest regions of the psyche.

The study of religion is a uniquely illuminating window onto human culture. Virtually universal, religion reveals many polarities, from the publicly expressed to the intensely private, motivating broad cultural and political events and giving expression to the depths of the psyche, both individual and collective. Religion has been the inspiration for the most saintly acts, and the justification for the most heinous. Its study captures the human dimension of history, what drives and inspires man in his deepest core.

An overview of the world's religions inspires an appreciation for both the commonalities and the remarkable diversity in different cultures' approaches to fundamental human questions. We can learn from the common ground shared by disparate traditions that stands as testament to our common humanity, as well as from the remarkable variety of ways in which the Absolute has been conceived.

In the context of this book, religion and spirituality (by which people often mean a more personal, direct experience of the transcendent) are seen as integral and overlapping facets of man's natural relationship with the sacred, which has always included side by side both the tendency to create structured institutions and ritual observances, and the interior, individual transcendent experience of the devotee and mystic.

A few words are in order here about the portrayal of Africa in this book. Though the aim is to fully represent the major developments in the history of world religion, the historian and scholar is dependent upon documentation to make her case. In order to be visible to historians, cultures must have written records, however African cultures were largely oral and did not always lend themselves to historical documentation in a Western sense. In addition, it is a regrettable fact that study of African religion among Western scholars is a relatively new field, and has yet to benefit from a comprehensive body of scholarly research. Thus, the relative sparseness of entries on Africa is not an intentional omission, but a reflection of the current incomplete state of scholarship.

This book focuses on events of particular significance to an English-speaking audience. Thus, the focal point shifts during different periods in the course of our survey: for example, during the prehistoric era key developments take place in Europe, Asia, and Australia, during the Axial Age in the great civilizations of Greece, the Middle East, India, and China. Though the greatest effort has been made to paint a comprehensive picture, the story of religion for English speakers is unavoidably seen through the lens of such events as the Renaissance, the Protestant Reformation, and the Colonial era—events that shaped the very perception of history in the Western world. Thus, in these periods the focus is often directed to these events.

How to Use This Book

The topic of world religion is particularly well suited to an illustrated timeline format, allowing a graphic depiction of parallel events around the world. Indeed, one of the most striking insights revealed by a comparative survey of world religion is the parallelism in the emergence of ideas, for example in the Axial Age period 800-200 B.C.

This book spans major world religious events from the prehistoric era beginning around 120,000 B.C. to the present day. It is divided into five major sections, each depicting a distinct era in the evolution of religious thought and practice. Each section contains a short introduction providing historical and cultural context for the events presented within.

The material is arranged in a chronological timeline format, consisting of images accompanied by text entries that discuss key personalities, events, and ideas, as well as their cultural relevance and the historical forces underlying them. To make the comparison by region even more clear, entries are color-coded by continent. Sidebars appear throughout the text, focusing in more detail on topics of particular interest.

It is hoped that this highly accessible book will provide an entertaining and informative visual tour through some of religious history's most inspiring moments.

Color Key

= Europe

= North America

= Asia

= Africa

= South America

= Australia

Prehistoric and Primal Religion: The Dawn of the Sacred, 120,000–3000 B.C.

When did religion begin? The answer seems to be that as long as there have been human beings, there has been a sense of the sacred giving rise to expression in myth, ritual, and art. Indeed, evidence of religion is found along with the earliest signs of human culture, dating from as early as the Middle Paleolithic period of the Neanderthals upward of 100,000 years ago and finding fuller expression in the Cro-Magnon society of the Upper Paleolithic from about 35,000 years ago. Early man lived as hunter-gatherers in small clans, first in caves and later settling in villages in the Mesolithic period around 10,000 years ago. It is in this context that the earliest ideas and practices relating to the sacred emerged.

The essential function of religion for early man was connecting the visible world to the invisible realm of powerful spirits and forces of nature, as evidenced in the remnants of sacred sites that form our earliest clues about what they might have believed in. We can't possibly know for certain what was in the minds of man so long ago, but we can infer from the archaeological evidence. That evidence tells us that ritual formed a central aspect of early man's religious life in the form of elaborate burials, ceremonies to call animal spirits for the hunt, and the shaman's techniques of ecstasy, healing, and divination.

Man differs from the animals in that he has the ability to conceive of an abstract past and future, which is different from the concrete reality of the present. We may speculate that humankind's ability (perhaps a mixed blessing) to wonder about the past, speculate about the future, and worry about what lay ahead marked the beginnings of belief in the life of the soul beyond death, and the reality of gods and spirits who control such forces as the weather, the migration of animals, and later, the creation of the world. Equally central to early man's religious sensibility appears to be a sense of wonder at the grandeur of the cosmos, embodied in the night sky with its lofty choreography of heavenly bodies, the orderly procession of the seasons with the miraculous return of spring each year, and the delicate balance of the interdependent community of life in which ancient man moved and upon which he depended for his sustenance.

Myths were the earliest attempts to form a coherent account of the cosmos and were passed along in the form of stories and rituals. Myth can be thought of as a collective expression of society, stemming from the imagination and deep symbolic realms of the psyche. Though no written records exist at this early period, we gather from the evidence that remains that the Australian aborigines, for example, told stories of the "Dreamtime"—the eternal realm of being that is the source of creation—and the "Rainbow Serpent" spirit of water who carves out gullies and channels as he moves across the land. The rational attempt to create a logical set of creeds and propositions comes only later with the development of historical religions, concurrent with the invention of written texts (scriptures) and a class of priests, religious professionals dedicated to preserving and transmitting doctrine.

The earliest religious specialist was the shaman (from the word *saman*, "one who knows"), who entered an ecstatic trance through methods such as drumming, chanting, fasting, use of psychedelic plants, or by self-induced pain to journey to the realm of the spirits and to heal. A nearly universal cross-cultural figure in indigenous cultures, found on every continent with local variations, the shaman mediates between the ordinary world and the unseen world of the spirits. The shaman embodies within himself the functions of priest, magician, and prophet, roles that later come to be separated into distinct specializations in organized religions.

A special relationship between man and animal typifies prehistoric attitudes toward the sacred, and shows his intimate connection with the natural world. This is evident in the earliest paintings, dating from the Upper Paleolithic, which feature not human, but animal subjects, and may have been used as ritual preparation for the hunt. The extraordinary cave paintings of such places as Lascaux in their luminous beauty and immediacy convey this sense of communion with the animals.

Prehistoric religion is also notable for its veneration of the feminine principle, embodied in the figure of a goddess found very widely throughout Europe and Asia, especially in the form of small statuettes of rotund female figures such as the famous Venus of Willendorf, which most probably indicate ritual worship as a fertility figure. The primitive goddess is a true earth mother, a paean to the precious bounties of material abundance that must have been rare in the subsistence lifestyle of ancient peoples. This primal goddess is a very different type from the later goddesses of classical religions (such as the Greek), who portray a refinement of culturally feminine virtues such as chastity, purity, and ethereal delicacy.

The seeds of the later historical religions can be found in our ancestors' earliest responses to the mystery of the world around them. Far from becoming obsolete, the earliest expressions of the sacred form the wellspring of later religions. The primal sense of wonder and its intuitive expression in myth and ritual become the inspiration for organized religions later on, with their hierarchical institutions and abstract, logical formulations of God. We have not moved so far from our ancient ancestors as we might think in our responses to the unseen, and our common heritage grants us the possibility to find renewed inspiration in their expressions of the mysteries of life, death, and the beyond.

120,000–35,000 B.C. Middle Paleolithic Period

The hunter-gatherer culture of the Neanderthals, regarded as a separate species from modern man, flourishes in Europe and the Mediterranean. This Stone Age culture lives in caves and fashions skillful axes, awls, and scrapers out of flint. Neanderthal graves and feasting rituals are the first evidence of human religious activity. Discovery of charred bones and pierced skulls at Neanderthal sites suggest ritual feasting, possibly cannibalism, and sacrifice. Ritual treatment is indicated by single or groups of decapitated skulls found opened at the base to remove the brains. Bear skulls and bones found in charred cave niches may indicate a cult of the bear spirit.

50,000 B.C. Neanderthal tomb burial from La Chapelle aux Saints, France. Bodies are buried in crouching position with food offerings and flint tools, sometimes in East-West orientation, suggesting belief in afterlife.

40,000 B.C. Australia's Aboriginal spiritual world centers on "Dreamtime," an eternal reality inhabited by mythic gods of creation who shaped the land and created animals, people, and rules of society. Myths are told, dances and rituals performed to enter into the dreamtime. Abstract paintings on wood or bark (like emu dreaming painting, pictured) depict the Dreamtime landscape.

35,000–10,000 B.C. Upper Paleolithic Period

After the end of the last Ice Age, Cro-Magnon man emerges as the first modern human. This hunter-gatherer society practices ritualized burials under stone slabs with bone and shell ornaments and tools. Belief in the afterlife is indicated by bodies found covered with red pigment symbolizing blood. The first art emerges from this period in the form of cave paintings, stone carvings (petroglyphs) and molded figures. Found in France, Spain, and Southern Italy, detailed paintings of game animals such as bison, mammoths, and reindeer suggest a ritual function, invoking animal spirits for the hunt, or to embody their magical power.

20,000 B.C. Earliest known image of shaman is painted on cave wall in Les Trois Freres, France. Figure has eyes of an owl, beard and feet of a man, horns of a reindeer, paws of a bear, a horse's tail, and is perhaps engaged in a dance to call animal spirits.

First Depictions of Womankind

In the Paleolithic era, representations of women outnumber those of men. Carved images of a few inches in height, similar to the Venus of Willendorf, have been found over a wide area ranging from France to Siberia and are generally thought to be fertility idols, sharing similar exaggerated characteristics such as rounded bellies and breasts. Since Stone Age peoples lived by hunting and gathering, it's unlikely that normal women would have had the opportunity to become so fat. Thus, these idols may depict pregnant women cared for by their tribes, fed rich food and living sedentary lifestyles, though their true significance and uses remain mysterious. It seems clear, however, that this prehistoric female figure is not directly linked to later goddesses such as the Middle Eastern Inanna, who was identified with agriculture, yet to be developed.

Shamanism

Shamanism (from Siberian Tungus *saman*, "one who knows") may be considered the world's oldest spiritual practice and is nearly universal throughout indigenous cultures worldwide. The shaman, also known popularly as a "medicine man," may be called a "specialist in non-ordinary reality" (to use terminology that was coined by such scholars as Carlos Castaneda and Michael Harner) who goes into an ecstatic trance, and journeys to the realms of the spirits, working with them to bring about healing or to gain information, for example, about the movement of game animals. Thus, the shaman's art specializes in three activities: healing, magical flight, and divination. The shaman's ecstatic trance can be induced by a variety of methods, including drumming, chanting, fasting, the use of psychedelic substances such as the peyote cactus of Mexico, or self-induced pain such as walking on hot coals or lacerating the skin with knives.

20,000 B.C.

24,000 B.C. Palm-sized statue Venus of Willendorf is one of the earliest carved human figures. Long identified as a fertility idol with her round figure, pronounced sexual characteristics, and tiny arms and hands that press down on her upper breasts, as if nursing. Traces of red pigment on the original carving may have symbolized menstrual blood and lend credence to theory that it was used as a fertility talisman.

13,500 B.C. Prevailing theory holds that Paleo-Indians migrate via Bering land bridge from Siberia to North America at this time. Archaeological evidence, such as chipped stone spearheads in distinctive patterns, has been found at Clovis culture sites throughout North and Central America. Clovis culture (named for Clovis, New Mexico, where the first artifacts were discovered) has been widely regarded as the earliest Native American culture, dating from the end of the last Ice Age.

10,000 B.C. The Ice Age ends with a global rise in sea level and widespread catastrophic flooding. Thought by some scholars to be origin of the Mesopotamian Flood story, recorded in the Sumerian *Epic of Gilgamesh*, and the Old Testament story of Noah.

10,000–8000 B.C. Mesolithic Period

This era marks the shift from nomadic to village life. Fishing, use of tools such as the bow and arrow and the sickle shown here, and the reliance on dogs supports hunting and gathering in fixed locations. Round symbols of the sun and moon occur in stone carvings and artifacts along with veneration of stones and pillars, regarded as embodying spiritual forces, and signs of star and tree worship.

Neolithic Period

This period marks the beginning of agriculture and domestication of animals, including the goat, sheep, and pig. Technological advances occur in pottery, weaving, and sewing. The establishment of settled communities with great growth in population, permanent buildings, and wheeled carts takes place. The fertility goddess of the earlier hunter-gatherer cultures is more closely tied in this period to the agricultural cycle of the earth, and mythologies of the Dying and Rising Gods emerge in the Middle East, such as the Sumerian goddess Inanna.

5000 B.C.

6500 B.C. Çatal Hüyük, a complex of mud-brick buildings and shrines in central Turkey, is earliest evidence of religious activity in Anatolian region and one of the largest Neolithic sites. Large figures of goddesses giving birth, and animals such as leopards, bulls, and rams are modeled on shrine walls. Small stone and terra-cotta statues depict a goddess and male figures, sometimes accompanied by panthers and other animals. Dead are buried in pits within the settlement, and disembodied skulls seem to serve a ritual purpose. Central deity is a goddess who presides over animals and is accompanied by a consort—a bearded man on a bull—and a son, a young man riding a leopard. Images of mother goddesses and male-female pairs are found widely at sacred sites throughout the region. This society may have been relatively egalitarian, as no evidence of social hierarchy—kings or priests—has been found. Men and women appear to have had relatively equal social status.

3100 B.C. Neolithic temple complex of Stonehenge in England is built in several stages. Earliest phase consists of circular ditches and mounds built with antler picks surrounding site. Second and third phases take place over a thousand years starting c. 2100 B.C., during which several sets of stone monoliths are arranged in two incomplete concentric circles aligned with summer solstice sunrise, later rebuilt in two new concentric groups of upright monoliths with lintels. Actual function of site is unknown, though may have been used for sacrificial observance of winter solstice.

Classical Religions: Realms of the Gods, 3000–800 B.C.

Evidence suggests that organized religion developed for the first time around the middle of the fourth millennium B.C. along with the transition from village culture to urban settlements and the first cities, such as Lagash, Ur, and Nippur. Generally regarded as the first literate societies, the civilizations of Mesopotamia ("the land between the rivers")—Sumer, followed by the Akkadian Empire, Assyria, and Babylonia—sprang up in the fertile marshland between the Tigris and Euphrates rivers. The transition from local tribal groups and villages to settled cities and nations resulted in more specialized and developed forms of religion that reflected the new social and political structures.

Writing, perhaps the foremost technological achievement of the Mesopotamian cultures, first developed to keep accounting records of such things as surplus grain, gave rise in time to literature and the first recorded myths and epics such as the story of Gilgamesh (c. 1850 B.C.), the great Sumerian culture hero who is civilized by beer and women but fails to win immortality, and the *Enuma Elish* (c. 1800 B.C.), the Babylonian creation myth that tells of the messy creation of the world from the familial infighting of the gods.

Tremendous advances were also made in the sciences during this period, particularly in mathematics and astronomy, giving rise to more precise mastery of agricultural cycles. Presiding over these technologies was a class of priests, who evolved as religious functionaries, performing rituals and serving as custodians of sacred lore, which in time was recorded and became the basis of the first great religious scriptures.

These early cultures were theocracies that blended the mythic conception of deities and cosmic cycles with the earthly affairs of man below. The king was seen as an embodiment of the divine, working in concert with the gods to bring order and harmony to the realm.

Parallel developments soon followed in the major areas of world civilization. In China we find the earliest mythic and historical records of the Shang and Chou dynasties of the second millennium B.C. and the emergence of Taoist ideas of orderly patterns of change in nature forming the basis for the *Book of Changes* (*I Ching*). Concurrently in India we find the development of the earliest Hindu rituals, including the fire sacrifice to the *devas*, or gods of the natural world, reflected in the myths of the Vedas. In Egypt, the evolution of hieroglyphic writings and myths and rituals of the afterlife occur during this period. In Meso- and South America, advanced knowledge of astronomical cycles and a ritual calendar provided the basis for an advanced civilization. The beginnings of the Jewish tradition can also be found during this period, with the seminal figures of

Abraham and Moses, and later the Prophets, emerging from the heritage of the Mesopotamian cultures of the ancient Near East. Each of these cultures emerged in similar contexts (with the partial exception of the Jewish culture, which emerged in nomadic as well as urban settings): the surplus of agriculture led to settled, later urban, life with the bureaucracy of an organized state such as a system of taxation and division of labor.

This era also saw the development of the great pantheons of gods, who, it was often believed, lived in a highly bureaucratic and specialized domain upon which earthly life was modeled. Several common character types are found among these early deities, including the Sky God, the ultimate creator who presides over the laws of the universe. This deity was represented in the form of Indra, storm god of the ancient Vedas; Marduk, the Babylonian sun god; and the great Shang Ti or embodiment of Heaven of China.

The "mother goddess" retains a central place in these early pantheons, though she evolved from the primitive fertility goddess of the prehistoric period. She is by this time the goddess of agriculture who presides over the growing cycle of the year. One of her most enduring forms is in the Greek myth of Demeter and her daughter Persephone, which was the basis of the Eleusinian Mystery cult that lasted for nearly two thousand years.

Nature deities filled out the divine cast of these ancient cultures, and as personifications of natural forces such as sun, moon, planets, storm, wind, and fire, showed how dependent man was on the rhythms of nature, which still provided the template for order and change.

In this period there did not yet exist the kind of humanitarian religious ethic that defines the later historical religions such as Christianity, Confucianism, and Buddhism, which we have come to take for granted. Rather, the first formal law codes such as that of Babylonian king Hammurabi, which decreed the law of retaliation summed up by the maxim "an eye for an eye," provided a systematic order to social interaction, but one that assumed a stratified society in which duty was determined by one's social rank rather than the inalienable individual rights.

Overall, this age saw a great advance in culture and the beginnings of religion in an institutionally developed form. Many of the gods, myths, and scriptures of this ancient period continue to live on in our collective cultural memory, providing profound expressions of the mysteries of life that continue to inspire.

3000 B.C.
The art of writing develops in Sumer in form of cuneiform script incised on clay tablets. Earliest writing keeps accounts of grain and other goods. Later, myths and priestly ritual are recorded.

2800 B.C. Flourishing of the Indus Valley Civilization, indigenous culture of India, until 1800 B.C. Some Indus Valley traditions are incorporated into later Hinduism, such as ritual bathing, the sacred cow, and the goddess tradition. Samples of the still-undeciphered Indus Valley script exist on carved seals, such as the one shown here depicting a horned god, possibly an early form of the god Shiva, seated in the lotus position, which may indicate the existence of yogic techniques. One theory holds that this native civilization is culturally or militarily subsumed around 1800 B.C. by Indo-Europeans, authors of the Vedas, sacred texts of Hinduism.

Mesopotamian Civilization in the Middle East: 3100–1600 B.C.

City-states such as Lagash, Ur, and Nippur develop from the village culture in the fertile marshes between the Tigris and Euphrates rivers, and fight each other until the Sumerian kingdoms rise, followed by the Akkadian, Assyrian, and Babylonian kingdoms. Each city has its patron god who presides over a larger pantheon, worshipped by priests. Ziggurats are built as symbolic "stairways to heaven" and the art of astrology develops to track the movement of the divine heavenly bodies.

c. 2800 B.C. Chinese Emperor Fu Hsi, one of the legendary Three Emperors of Chinese mythology, is credited with bringing many aspects of culture to the Chinese people, such as writing. The trigrams, or patterns of broken and solid lines that form the basis of the *I Ching* (or *Book of Changes*), a classic manual of divination, are said to have appeared to him in a vision.

2494–2345 B.C. The Pyramid Texts, some of the oldest known writings, are composed in Egypt. A collection of ancient religious texts from the time of the Old Kingdom consisting mostly of inscriptions on the walls of pyramid tombs, they depict the Egyptian view of the afterlife and the ascent into the sky of the divine Pharaoh after death.

2300 B.C. *Shu Ching* (*Book of History*) is one of the Five Confucian Classics. The earliest of the Chinese historical chronicles, it covers the period from c. 2300 to c. 721 B.C. including the legendary Golden Age of the 3rd millennium, the purported Hsia dynasty (c. 2000–1500 B.C.), the Shang dynasty (1700–1027 B.C.), and the Western Chou dynasty (1027–771 B.C.), representing ideals of harmony and enlightened leadership by the emperor who embodies the Mandate of Heaven.

c. 2400 B.C. The myth of Osiris, fertility god and lord of the under-world, originates during this period. At the center of Egyptian religion is the concept of divine kingship; it is thought that after the king's death, he becomes Osiris. Osiris' festival, consisting of processions and nocturnal rites, are celebrated at the temple of Abydos, and an annual reenactment of his story occurs throughout Egypt.

The Myth of Osiris

As the story goes, Osiris is killed by the god Set who flings the 14 pieces of his corpse over Egypt. The goddess Isis, along with her sister Nephthys, gather all of the pieces, except for the phallus, and reassemble Osiris, binding his parts together with the wrappings of a mummy. Osiris comes alive again and remains in the underworld as ruler and judge. Isis and Osiris conceive a son, Horus, who kills Set and becomes the new king of Egypt. The myth of Osiris as Dying and Rising God spreads throughout the ancient world and influences Greco-Roman myths, such as the Greek Mystery cults, and the myth of Dionysus. It may also have indirectly inspired the tradition of Christianity.

2200–1500 B.C. Minoan civilization of Crete, an agricultural and trading society, worships goddess who encompasses aspects of fertility, hearth, and the underworld. She is often represented by serpents and may be connected to the male "Earthshaker" deity represented by a sun–bull who dies each autumn and returns each spring.

c. 1850 B.C. Written version of the *Epic of Gilgamesh* dates from this period. Gilgamesh, god–king of Uruk, pursues many heroic adventures with his rival Enkidu the wild man, who is tamed by the priestess–harlot Shamash. Ultimately, Gilgamesh fails at attaining immortality and is killed by a bull, arousing the grief of the people.

2000 B.C.

c. 1850 B.C. Abraham, patriarch of Judaism, is thought to have lived. As his story is told, he migrates from Ur after hearing the command of God to found a new nation in Canaan. Abraham receives a covenant from God that his descendants will prosper and inherit the land. He has a son, Ishmael, by the maidservant Hagar, and is later miraculously given a son, Isaac, by his barren wife Sarah. As a test of faith, Abraham is asked by God to sacrifice Isaac, but at the last minute God substitutes a ram for the boy. According to the Bible, Abraham lived to the age of 175.

1800 B.C. The *Enuma Elish* Babylonian creation myth is composed, telling of the creation of the world from a primal marsh by the mother–father gods Apsu and Tiamat, and their son Marduk, solar god who ascends to power by killing his parents.

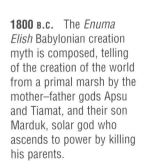

1700 B.C. According to tradition, the Jews arrive in Egypt, escaping famine in Israel.

The Afterlife in Ancient Egypt

The *Egyptian Book of the Dead* contains magical formulas intended to help the dead navigate the trials en route to the underworld. The heart of the deceased is weighed by Anubis against the standard of *ma'at* or truth, and the god Thoth records the results. If the heart weighs less than a feather, the deceased is allowed to go on; otherwise, the monster Ammit consumes the unworthy soul.

c. 1700 B.C. The Code of Hammurabi (1726–1686 B.C.), one of the earliest legal codes, is issued by the Babylonian king as an edict written in stone. Hammurabi writes these laws to please his gods, as the stele shows him in front of the sun god Shamash. The Code teaches the law of retribution and is a model for the Torah law of Moses, and the teaching "an eye for an eye" (Exodus 21:24). This is a cultural advance, which sets a limit on the extent of retribution allowed under the prior custom of tribal blood vendetta.

1580 B.C. The *Egyptian Book of the Dead* is composed in its earliest form. Its true title is the *Book of Going Forth by Day* and it's a funerary text which was first carved on the outside of the deceased's sarcophagus, later written on papyrus scrolls placed inside. The work, which changed over time, reached its finalized form around 1350 B.C.

1500 B.C. Hinduism: The composition of the Vedas: Rig, Sama, and Yajur by the Indo–European Aryans. The Vedas ("knowledge") contain revealed wisdom and are regarded as the core sacred texts of Hinduism, consisting of hymns, mantras (incantations), and ritual instructions for sacrificial rites of the Brahmin priests. Rituals are meant to supplicate the *devas*, or gods who are personifications of natural forces such as Indra the storm god and Agni the god of fire. The Vedas at this time are oral texts and are memorized; at some point, unknown, they are written down, but remain an essentially oral tradition.

1500 B.C.

1500 B.C. Greek Eleusinian Mysteries, held annually at Eleusis, near Athens, begin about this time and continue for around 2000 years. These initiation ceremonies into the cult of the fertility goddess Demeter and her daughter Persephone consist of purification, procession, and reenactment of the myth during which initiates drink a wine potion called *kykeon* that may have contained psychedelic herbs, are shown the secrets of Demeter, learn the mysteries of life after death, and are then sworn to silence. The Eleusinian Mysteries are the most important of the Greek mystery cults, and by their heyday in the early centuries A.D. have great cultural impact on the Greco–Roman world, including many leading intellectuals such as Sophocles, Herodotus, and Plutarch.

The Mystery of the Seasons

Persephone is kidnapped by Hades, god of the underworld. While searching for her daughter, the distraught Demeter neglects her duties, causing the dry season to fall upon the land and make the crops barren—winter. Persephone is eventually returned to the realm of the living, and spring blooms. Unfortunately, having eaten 6 pomegranate seeds that Hades had given her, Persephone is bound to return to the underworld for several months of each year, ensuring the return of winter. The Mysteries celebrate the return of Persephone, and thus the renewed life of the plants and nature.

c. 1250 B.C.
According to tradition, Moses leads the Hebrews out of exile in Egypt. First books of the Torah (Old Testament) are composed.

1200 B.C.
The Olmecs build the first pyramids and temples in Central America in south–central Mexico.

The Olmec Civilization

The Olmecs are the mother culture of all later Mesoamerican civilizations and predominate in the region 1200–400 B.C. Notable contributions include developing a hieroglyphic script and a mathematical calendar that is

the basis of their cosmology. They also invent the ballgame that is central to Mesoamerican religious practices, a ritual contest, sometimes a matter of life or death for the contestants, that sometimes involves putting a small ball through a high stone hoop without using the hands. Many Olmec statues depict a "were–jaguar"—half infant, half jaguar—or colossal heads, both of which are thought to have spiritual meanings.

1220–1200 B.C.
Judaism: According to biblical tradition, Joshua is appointed successor to Moses after the exodus from Egypt and leads the Israelite army in invading Canaan. He captures the city of Jericho and surrounding region, dividing it among the 12 tribes of Israel, thus establishing a territory for the Israelites.

c. 1100 B.C.
Compilation of the Chinese classic *I Ching (Book of Changes)*, by leaders of the Chou dynasty. These developments clarify and expand the system of the *bagua* or trigrams and evolve the *I Ching* into a comprehensive philosophy that greatly influences the literature and government policy of the Chou dynasty (c. 1122–256 B.C.).

The Philosophy of Yin-Yang

By the time of the Chou dynasty the early Chinese tradition of divination from patterns of cracks on heated tortoise shells and bones has evolved into the scheme of the Eight Trigrams, or *bagua*. These patterns of solid and broken lines represent the positive, male principle of yang, and the negative, female principle of yin and are seen to exist in different proportions in all phenomena. The trigrams are combined to make 64 hexagrams, representing all possible combinations. The classic emblem shows the 8 trigrams arranged in an octagon with the symbol of yin-yang in the center, representing the source of creation and depicting the dynamic nature of the two principles of creation, each containing the seed of its opposite. Starting at the top and moving clockwise, the trigrams represent moving water and moon, thunder, earth, mountain, fire and sun, wind and wood, heaven, and still water.

c. 1000 B.C. The Atharva Veda is composed. This is the latest of the Veda texts, which contains technical instructions for the sacrificial rites of the Brahmins.

c. 1010–970 B.C. Judaism: King David rules the kingdom of Israel and conquers Jerusalem, which is made the political and spiritual center of the land. David is Israel's second king, succeeding the troubled reign of Saul (c. 1021–1000 B.C.) and surviving the former king's jealous attempt to kill him. Messianic expectations surround the legend of King David and continue into New Testament traditions.

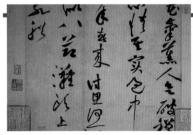

1000–500 B.C. *Chih Ching* (*Book of Odes*), the first major collection of Chinese poetry, is composed. One of the Five Confucian Classics, its poems contain historical, mythic, and religious material, and are sung at ceremonial occasions and sacrifices.

957 B.C. The First Temple in Jerusalem is completed during the reign of King Solomon, son of David (990–922 B.C.). It's built on Mount Moriah, the Temple Mount, believed to be where Abraham built the altar on which to sacrifice his son Isaac. Home to the Ark of the Covenant, the central religious object of Israel, which thus unifies the monarchy with religion and is a symbol of unity for the Israelite tribes.

Jerusalem

The holy city of three faiths, Jerusalem is of key importance to the three monotheistic religions of Judaism, Christianity, and Islam, which all regard Abraham as their patriarch and share the historical tradition of the Old Testament. Jews identify the city with King David and the establishment of the Jewish homeland. The city figures prominently in Jewish worship and is mentioned during the services of Passover and Yom Kippur. The remains of the western wall of the Second Temple, known as the "wailing wall," are still a focus of prayer for many observant Jews, and the idea of the return to Jerusalem has a powerful influence in Jewish thought. For Christians, Jerusalem is identified with the events of Christ's last days, including the Last Supper, trial, crucifixion, and resurrection. In Islam, Jerusalem is revered for its identification with the Old Testament prophets, and was the first direction of prayer before Mecca was established. It is regarded as the location where Muhammad began his ascension to heaven on the magical steed Buraq in his night journey or *Mi'raj*.

c. 900 B.C. Pre-Inca temple of Chavin de Huantar built by the Chavin civilization. This earliest known Andean culture displays elements of later Andean religion, such as the worship of jaguars, hawks, and snakes. Archaeological evidence suggests use of hallucinogenic herbs, temple sacrifices, and shamanic techniques meant to commune with the animal spirits and forces of fertility.

c. 950 B.C. Judaism: The Old Testament books of the Pentateuch are composed in their early versions. The Pentateuch, from Greek "five containers," is also known as the Tanakh in Hebrew. The Five Books of Moses, include Genesis, Exodus, Leviticus, Numbers and Deuteronomy. Scholars identify 4 strands of authorship that compose the Pentateuch: the Yahwist (J), Elohist (E), Deuteronomist (D), and Priestly (P). This earliest strand represents the Yahwist (J) voice, named because God is referred to as Yahweh. One example of these differing strands is that of the two accounts of creation in Genesis—the latter (2:5) is the older, Yahwist source; the earlier (1:1) is thought to be a later account, written around the 6th century B.C. by the Priestly source.

c. 926 B.C. Judaism: The Kingdom of Israel is divided into Northern (Israel) and Southern (Judah) states, when the Northern tribes secede in protest of King Rehoboam's extravagance and high taxes.

c. 870 B.C. Prophet Elijah is credited with saving the Jewish faith from the corruption of worshipping the Canaanite god Baal. Elijah appears during the reign of King Ahab and his pagan wife Jezebel and denounces Baalism, challenging the prophets of Baal to a contest. Yahweh's superiority is demonstrated by fire on Elijah's altar. Baal and his worship are thus banished from Israel. Elijah is also recognized as a prophet in Islam.

Historical Religion: The Axial Age and the Age of Empire, 800 B.C.–1500 A.D.

This era begins with a pivotal stage in the development of world religions, in many ways defining religious values as we know them today. This is the "Axial Age" (800–200 B.C.), a notion coined by German philosopher Karl Jaspers, referring to the idea that this era was an "axis" for the development of world culture, setting the standard by which future generations would evaluate their own cultural and religious ideals. It is the period in which the great classical systems of thought arose in India, China, the Middle East, and the Greco-Roman world. In each of these major areas of civilization we find strikingly parallel developments, independent of direct communication between these cultures, which we can only attribute to similar social and cultural dynamics in each region.

Many of the great religions emerged during this period, both those with a single founding figure at their center such as Buddhism, Zoroastrianism, and Confucianism, and those that expressed cultural traditions, such as Classical Greek philosophy and Taoism. Among the influential figures of this time were Zoroaster, Buddha, Mahavira (founder of the Jain religion), Confucius, Lao Tzu (traditional originator of Taoism), Elijah (the great Jewish prophet), and the great Greek philosophers Socrates, Plato, and Aristotle.

The signature religious development in the Axial Age was the articulation of a universal humanitarian ethic based on the ideal of compassion, or brotherly love, and expressed in distinctive ways in each religion. In the Judeo-Christian tradition, it was expressed in the Golden Rule, "love thy neighbor as thyself," which first appeared in the rabbinic tradition of Judaism and later became the center of Jesus' teaching. In India, we find the development of the idea of ahimsa or nonviolence in the Hindu tradition, and the ideal of universal compassion articulated in the bodhisattva figure of Buddhism. In China, two great philosophies were articulated: Taoism by Lao Tzu, who expressed the universal ethics of *wu-wei* or noninterference in personal and civic life, and Confucianism by Confucius, who articulated the ideal of the gentleman (*chün-tzu*) who embodied the notion of humanity (*jen*), understood as brotherly love. In Greece such notions as universal ideals of virtue (e.g., Plato's idea of the Good) were explored by philosophers.

The importance of the individual was an equally unprecedented development of the era. Literature of the Axial Age shifts attention from the nobility, who inherited their status, to the intellectual elite and to the person endowed with free will and moral conscience based on compassion and reason. Rather than focusing on ritual tradition or clan allegiances, humankind appears to reach a kind of existential self-awareness during this period, seeking salvation from death and the uncertainty of the hereafter through philosophical reflection and rational inquiry. This development is reflected in the great religious scriptures of this era that have become timeless classics, such as the Tao Te Ching of Taoism, the Hindu Upanishads, and the Torah books of Judaism.

Axial Age ideas reflected widespread changes in social conditions throughout the world's major civilizations. Ideas of political and cultural unity emerged in an era marked by strife as small, warring feudal states created constantly shifting borders and social chaos and an attitude of ritualistic rigidity marked religious practice. The great teachers, visionaries of a new concept of human perfection, crossed borders proclaiming the ideal of universal love to counteract the problems of the day.

Feudal societies with their strict ideas of social classes and clan-based codes of ethics were gradually superseded by the emergence of the great empires, making possible the widespread acceptance of new ethical and spiritual ideas. The universal ideals of the Axial Age were the necessary moral counterpart of a unified empire with its extensive bureaucracy. These cultural developments laid the foundation for the Roman Empire and the Roman Catholic Church, the Indian Mauryan dynasty and Mahayana Buddhism, and the Han dynasty in China, which implemented the Confucian state. It's interesting to note that it was the rise of a monetary economy, mercantile trade, and the resulting autonomy and mobility of a growing "middle class" that allowed the Axial Age religions, with their teachings of individual moral conscience, altruistic ethics, and egalitarian humanism to take root.

The period following the Axial Age (800–200 B.C.) may be called the Age of Empire. This era saw the further development of the great religions, which tended to become more institutionalized, forming orthodoxies that focused on correct doctrine and ritual observance, such as the Roman Catholic Church. Concurrently, the esoteric and mystical branches of the great religions developed during this time: the Kabbalistic tradition of Judaism, the Gnostic tradition of Christianity, the Sufi tradition in Islam, the Tantric tradition in Hinduism and Buddhism, as well as comparable developments in China such as Taoist alchemical practices.

From the time of the Axial Age until 1500 A.D., which marks the approximate beginning of the Protestant Reformation, many significant historical developments occurred that have shaped the course of religion. These include: the conquest of Alexander the Great; the flourishing and decline of the Roman Empire, which supported Christianity; the Crusades; the Inquisition; the Jewish Diaspora of 1492; the Renaissance; the flowering of the Islamic empires; and the rise of the great Chinese Confucian dynasties. These events laid the groundwork for the modern era, and we are still working out many of their ramifications in the present day. It appears that we have not yet completely mastered the teachings of universal brotherly love given to us by the great spiritual teachers over two millennia ago, though perhaps we are gradually drawing closer to their realization.

c. 800 B.C. Hindu sages compose the early Brahmanas, Aranyakas, and Upanishads—the root philosophical texts of Hinduism, considered commentaries on the Vedas. Brahmanas ("exposition of the sacred word") and Aranyakas ("forest books") record the secret explanation of the Vedic sacrificial rites. The Upanishads ("to sit down near") record dialogues between gurus and disciples practicing the path of yoga and meditation in secluded retreats. The later 6 classical schools of Indian philosophy consider themselves commentaries on the Upanishads. Composition of later Aranyakas, Brahmanas, and Upanishads continues for several centuries.

c. 750 B.C. Judaism: Dating of the Elohist source (E)—one of the 4 strands of biblical narrative in the Pentateuch as identified by scholars, named because God is called Elohim rather than Yahweh. Elohist (E) sections are thought to have been written in the Northern Kingdom of Israel, presenting a northern setting for the events of Genesis. They portray God as more abstract and removed from direct human experience, placing greater emphasis on prophecy as the means by which God communicates with mankind. At some point the traditions of the Yahwist (J) and Elohist (E) sources were merged, and both are integral to the Pentateuch account.

800 B.C.

c. 750 B.C.
Judaism: Prophet Amos is first "literary prophet" to have a book of the Bible named for him. He foretells the destruction of the Northern Kingdom of Israel and the apocalypse.

742 B.C.
Judaism: The Old Testament Book of Isaiah is begun. Hebrew prophet Isaiah has a vision in which he's charged to condemn the Jews for their fall from righteousness and to watch the Jewish nation perish; a message met with resistance and ridicule. Isaiah stresses the ethical duties of the Covenant. The Christian tradition draws heavily from Isaiah, seeing evidence there of the prophesy of Christ as Messiah.

722 B.C. Judaism: Israel, the Northern Kingdom, is invaded by the army of Assyrian King Sargon II and residents are exiled, causing the 10 Northern Tribes to be lost to history, according to biblical tradition.

c. 700 B.C. Greek classical religion flourishes for 17 centuries from the time of Homer (author of the *Odyssey* and the *Iliad*) to the reign of emperor Julian in the 4th century A.D. Greek ideas about the divine had great influence on the ancient world, including the Roman Empire and Christianity. Unlike later Western religions, Greek religion was typified by the belief in many gods depicted in human form with a focus on mythology and ritual observance rather than dogma. Zeus, Demeter, Athena, Apollo, and many other gods lived on Mount Olympus, where they engaged in exploits of love and war, and sometimes involved themselves in human affairs, for good or ill.

c. 620 B.C. Judaism: The Old Testament Books of Deuteronomy, Joshua, Judges 1 and 2, Samuel, and 1 and 2 Kings are composed by the author(s) scholars identify as the Deuteronomist source (D) during the Deuteronomic Reform, about 35 years before the destruction of the first temple, when Israel had been under Assyrian domination for a generation. At a time when ritual observance had become lax, the Deuteronomist voice stresses adherence to the covenant with Yahweh, and the status of Israel as God's chosen nation.

c. 628–551 B.C. Life of Zoroaster (Zarathustra) Iranian prophet and founder of Zoroastrianism. The first hymns of the Avesta, the Gathas, are composed by him.

Zoroastrianism

This ancient Persian religion is founded by priest and prophet Zoroaster, who has a vision of Ahura Mazda ("Wise Lord"), the Supreme deity who created the universe and two opposing spirits: Spenta Mainyu, embodying goodness, truth, light, and life, and Angra Mainyu, embodying evil, falsehood, darkness, and destruction. The history of the world is the result of the conflict between the two opposing principles. The faith holds that Ahura Mazda will reward good actions and punish bad ones. Upon death, an individual's soul must be judged by Ahura Mazda, and is accordingly sent to a paradise or a hell. Zoroaster retains the traditional Persian custom of fire sacrifice, tended by priests, called Magi. In his lifetime, Zoroaster converts the king Vishtaspā and his teachings spread throughout the ancient Near East, influencing later monotheisms of Judaism, Christianity, and Islam. The faith survives today among the Parsis of India.

c. 599–527 B.C. Life of Mahāvīra ("Great Hero") Vardhamāna, founder and reformer of Jainism. His story and teachings have much in common with Buddha, and represent the same social climate in India—a questioning of the authority of the Brahmins, or priestly caste, by the upwardly mobile warrior, or *kṣatriya,* caste. Tradition holds that Mahāvīra was a prince who renounced the world to become a monk, and practicing a rigorous ascetic discipline, attained enlightenment and freedom from rebirth. His followers regarded him as the 24th and final saint or *Tīrthaṅkara* in the Jain lineage. Though there

had been Jain teachers before, it seems that Mahāvīra led a renaissance of the tradition, and is thus popularly regarded as the founder of the Jain faith. Jain doctrine teaches nonviolence, practiced in such forms as vegetarianism and vows of renunciation of such things as greed and sexual gratification.

580–500 B.C. Traditional dates of Lao Tzu ("old master"), Chinese sage and legendary author of the Tao Te Ching, a seminal Taoist text. Although many scholars question the dating and historical identity of Lao Tzu, as well as the fact that the Tao Te Ching was written by a single author, the old master is honored as a saint and philosopher by later Chinese tradition and regarded as the founder of Taoism.

597 B.C.
The Persian King Nebuchadnezzar captures Jerusalem and deports the Jews to exile in Babylon. In 587 he destroys the Temple and the City of Jerusalem. The exile ends in 538 when conquering Persian King Cyrus the Great allowed Jews to return to the Holy Land.

Taoism

A native tradition of China, encompassing ancient folk beliefs and rituals, Taoism honors the spirits of earth and ancestors and incorporates physical, ritual, and alchemical techniques in the pursuit of immortality. Its seminal philosophical texts are the Tao Te Ching of Lao Tzu, and the *Chuang Tzu* by the sage of the same name who lived a century or so after Lao Tzu. Taoist ideals center around the idea of the Tao: the invisible order of nature, exemplified in the movements of the heavens and found in particular in water, the paramount symbol of the Tao. The *yin-yang* symbol of interlocking light and dark circles indicates the dynamic harmony in the forces of nature, and this theory was applied to all areas of life, including medicine, politics and philosophy. The model of Taoist tradition is the sage who embodies a quality of "nonactivity" (*wu-wei*), holding the point of balance around which the world finds harmony. Though the Tao Te Ching was originally written as a guide for rulers, Taoism developed over the centuries into a widespread popular movement, spreading esoteric techniques for attaining immortality and forming diverse religious societies, which sometimes threatened the power of the government, as in the 2nd century A.D. uprising of the Yellow Turban sect.

563–483 B.C.
Life of Gautama
Buddha.

551–479 B.C. Life of Confucius or K'ung Fu-tzu, teacher and philosopher of social reform in China. Legend holds that he grows up poor, the fatherless son of a distantly aristocratic family, whose mother struggles to provide him an education. Confucius lives at a time of great social upheaval in China, during the breakdown of the great feudal powers, and his lifelong vision is to teach the principles of good society to his countrymen. To this end, he spends his life advising rulers of the small, warring states that had emerged in the wake of feudal breakdown, and gathers about him a group of disciples, 72 of which are regarded as his closest.

Buddhism

Although Buddhism eventually spreads to encompass much of Asia and develops into many different schools, the Buddhist tradition begins with Siddhartha Gautama, a prince of the Sakya clan in Northeast India in the 5th century B.C. The legend of his life states that as a young man, he renounces his life of privilege and seeks the answer to the suffering of mankind: old age, sickness, and death, which strike rich and poor alike. After practicing many ascetic techniques in the Hindu tradition, and nearly starving himself, Siddhartha, in meditation under the Bodhi tree, has the insight that confers enlightenment, and freedom from rebirth and its attendant suffering: that all things, including the self, are impermanent, simply a combination of parts that arise and decay in due time. There is thus no permanent soul or self (*ātman*), as Hindu doctrine holds. Upon attaining this truth, Siddhartha Gautama becomes the Buddha ("Awakened One") and spends the remainder of his life walking around the towns and cities of Northern India preaching his message of liberation. He gathers around him a group of disciples who take monastic vows, and the Buddhist *sangha*, or monastic order, is formed.

The Buddha is a social reformer of the Hindu caste system, proclaiming that all people, regardless of caste, can attain liberation. Early Buddhism, known as Hinayana ("lesser vehicle") centers on the monastic path of being a monk or nun, and the rigorous meditation needed to become an *arhat*, one who attains nirvana: the cessation of the self from future rebirth. As the Buddhist tradition develops, a more universal form of Buddhism, the Mahayana ("greater vehicle"), arises in the early centuries A.D. in conjunction with the consolidation of the Indian Empire under the Mauryan dynasty. Mahayana Buddhism develops the ideal of the bodhisattva—the aspiring "Buddha in training" who, out of deep compassion, postpones his own passage into nirvana in order to help all living beings attain liberation. Lay people as well as monks could become bodhisattvas, thus broadening the attainability of Buddhahood. Buddhism spreads in the following centuries from India to Central Asia, China, Japan, Sri Lanka, and Southeast Asia, becoming, in its heyday in the late 1st millennium A.D., one of the world's most popular religions.

Confucianism

In many ways resembling more an ethical philosophy than an organized religion, Confucianism nevertheless comes to be the dominant institutional force in Chinese history from its adoption as state religion under Emperor Wu of the Han dynasty in the 2nd century B.C., until the establishment of the Republic of China in the 20th century. For most of Chinese history, Confucian principles determine every branch of society: government, in the person of the emperor and his bureaucracy, education, law, and the rituals of private and civic life. Confucian philosophy centers around the principle of *jen*, translated as "love" or "humanity," which is the highest moral aim for a "gentleman" (*chün-tzu*), a term that Confucius took from its feudal context denoting an aristocratic birth, and applied to any person of good moral character. *Jen* represents the value of *tao*, or the underlying order of harmony. But whereas the Taoist school tends to find balance in the natural world and individual mysticism, Confucianism finds harmony in the social sphere, man's rightful place. As Confucius says in the *Analects*, "One cannot herd together with birds and beasts. If I am not to be a man among other men, then what am I to be? If the Way (*tao*) prevailed in the world, I should not be trying to alter things" (*Sources of Chinese Tradition,* compiled by William T. de Bary and Irene Bloom).

538 B.C. The Babylonian Exile ends with Cyrus the Great's conquest of Palestine, giving the Jews permission to return to the Holy Land. The Second Temple is built in Jerusalem.

470–399 B.C. Life of Socrates, Athenian philosopher and teacher of Plato. Widely regarded as the father of moral philosophy in the West, and a foundational figure for the Western philosophical tradition generally, he develops the Socratic method, a dialectic method of inquiry that identifies and eliminates contradictions through a process of questioning. No writing from the master survives, and he is known only from accounts of his countrymen, such as Plato and Aristotle. Tradition

holds that he runs a school of philosophy, and that he is tried and found guilty by the civic authorities of Athens for impiety and corruption of youth, due to his questioning of the common practices of civic piety. He is sentenced to death by the poison hemlock.

c. 483 B.C. First Buddhist Council in India. Buddhist tradition records that during the first rainy season after the death of Gautama Buddha, the community of Buddhist monks, represented by 500 *arhats* (monks who had attained nirvana, or liberation) gathered at Rajagriha to recite the corpus of teachings, including the Buddha's sermons (*sūtras*) and the monastic rule (*vinaya*). At this time, the teachings existed in a purely oral form, and were preserved by memorization.

c. 450 B.C. Judaism: Approximate dating for the Priestly source (P) of the Pentateuch, which constitutes large portions of the books of Genesis, Exodus, and Numbers. This final strand is composed by Temple priests of Israel after the destruction of the First Temple in 586 B.C. and finalized some time before its rebuilding in 450 B.C. The Priestly source (P) emphasizes the holiness code of temple worship and the priesthood as the ritual center of purity and the strength of Israel. The grand account of creation that opens Genesis (1:1–2:4) is attributed to the Priestly source (P).

c. 400 B.C. Judaism: The Old Testament book Song of Songs is finalized. Though it's traditionally ascribed to Solomon, historical evidence suggests that it is a compilation of oral tradition composed in the style of Near Eastern love poetry, with sensuous images and metaphors that were later interpreted in religious terms.

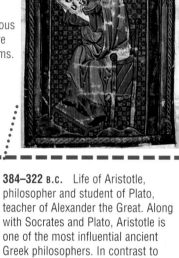

427–347 B.C. Life of Plato, writer, philosopher, founder of the Academy in Athens, student of Socrates, and teacher of Aristotle. He writes a number of influential works, notably the *Dialogues,* and teaches a form of metaphysical dualism, which claims that the world perceived by the senses and imagination is illusory and inferior to the true world evident to the intellect, the world of pure forms. Plato greatly influences later Western theological ideas, such as those of Plotinus and the Gnostics, as well as early Christian thought, and is rediscovered in Europe during the Renaissance flowering of humanism.

384–322 B.C. Life of Aristotle, philosopher and student of Plato, teacher of Alexander the Great. Along with Socrates and Plato, Aristotle is one of the most influential ancient Greek philosophers. In contrast to Plato, Aristotle emphasized knowledge gained from the senses. He lays the groundwork for the scientific method in the West and writes widely on natural science, philosophy, and government. Aristotelian methods become influential in the Christian church during the Middle Ages, when theologians such as Peter Abelard and Anselm of Canterbury make logic rather than dogmatic authority a requirement of theology.

c. 380 B.C. The Second Council of Buddhism is held at Vaishali in India, during which a dispute arises between two factions of monks over how strictly the monastic rule of the *Vinaya* should be observed. Among the points disputed are whether it's permissible for monks to store salt in a horn or to drink buttermilk after meals. It is widely believed that this dispute is a key cause of a schism in the early monastic community between the more liberal group, the Mahāsaṅghika school, and the Sthaviravāda school, which is more conservative.

c. 371–289 B.C. Life of Mencius (Meng Tzu) in China. Known as the "second sage," he's the foremost developer of Confucian thought who establishes the Confucian school. His teachings are recorded in the book *Mencius.* Like Confucius, Mencius is the son of a noble family who lost his father at a young age. Mencius devotes himself to study and becomes a teacher and political advisor to rulers, instructing them in the philosophy of humanity (*jen*) during the Warring States period, a time of social upheaval. Mencius emphasizes the duty of the ruler toward his subjects to provide both economic and educational support and advocates for the rights of the common people. He develops the Confucian doctrine of humanity stating that human nature is innately good. Like Confucius, Mencius does not meet with great acceptance by the nobility during his lifetime and spends his final years teaching students.

c. 369–286 B.C. Life of Chuang Tzu in China, foremost interpreter of Taoism and the teachings of Lao Tzu. Contemporary of Mencius, the great Confucian scholar, Chuang Tzu's text bearing his name is second only to the Tao Te Ching in importance, and is more comprehensive in its scope. He puts more emphasis on refuting the positions of the rival schools of Confucianism and Mohism. His interpretation of Taoism stresses the relativity of all human values, and the constant change of things against the backdrop of the eternal and formless tao. It is with the work of Chuang Tzu that Taoism takes its place among the great philosophical schools of China.

334 B.C. Alexander the Great invades Persia at the Battle of Granicus and in 333 B.C. defeats King Darius III at the Battle of Issus. Shortly afterward Alexander conquers the Persian capital Persepolis and tradition holds that the Zoroastrian Avesta, written in gold ink, is destroyed along with the imperial archives. Before Alexander's death in 323 B.C. the Macedonian Empire covers much of the known world, including Greece, Persia, Syria, and Egypt. Alexander's reign ushers in the Hellenistic period, a time of great flowering of religious ideas. The city of Alexandria is founded in Egypt, and under the reign of Ptolemy II at the beginning of the 3rd century B.C. becomes a center of learning in the ancient world until the late 4th century A.D.

300–230 B.C. Life of Hsün Tzu, one of the three great classical Confucian scholars, known by his work of the same name. He's responsible for elaborating on and systematizing the work of Confucius and Mencius, and thus for the continuation of the Confucian school. He holds the view that human nature is naturally evil and virtue can only be achieved by cultivation. This is opposite to the view of Mencius, who held that human nature was naturally good. With the rise of the Neo-Confucian movement in the 10th century Hsün Tzu loses favor to the interpretation of Mencius.

c. 300 B.C. Tradition holds that the great library of Alexandria is founded during the reign of Ptolemy II of Egypt, building on the work of his father Ptolemy I, who built the temple of the Muses, or Musaion. The library is the largest in the world, containing up to 500,000 papyrus scrolls, copied from the collections of great scholars of the day, and drawing seekers of learning from all over the ancient world.

300 B.C. The epic poem *Ramayana* (*"Story of Rama"*), attributed to the poet Valmiki, is composed in Sanskrit. The story relates the journey of Prince Rama of the kingdom of Ayodhya who, through intrigue, is exiled to the forest with his brother Laksmana, and beautiful wife Sita. While in exile, the demon king Ravana abducts Sita and carries her to his far-off palace of Lanka. Rama and his companions, including the loyal monkey-general Hanuman, set out to rescue her and encounter many adventures along the way. The *Ramayana* is much-beloved in India, and is retold in popular culture. Rama is considered a divine incarnation of the Hindu god Vishnu, and the epic deals with themes of religious duty, good and evil, and the contrasting values of kingship and spiritual asceticism.

c. 250 B.C. The first versions of the *Septuagint*, Greek translation of the Old Testament from Hebrew, is completed, intended for the Greek-speaking Jewish community in Egypt. The name derives from the legend that 70 (*septuaginta*: Latin "70") learned scholars from the 12 tribes of Israel completed the work. The translation of the Pentateuch dates from this period; the remainder of the Old Testament was probably translated in the mid-2nd century B.C.

Ashoka, the Buddhist Emperor

Ashoka (reigned c. 265–238 B.C.), the greatest emperor of the Mauryan dynasty, unifies the Indian subcontinent through military conquest. Upon his victory, he renounces violence and proclaims a rule by the Buddhist principles of *dharma* (religious truth and ethics such as compassion, truthfulness, and self-restraint) and sends missionaries to Sri Lanka, Central Asia, and Afghanistan to spread the Buddhist teachings. He erects rock pillars at sites around the empire inscribed with edicts containing Buddhist principles. He supports Buddhism by sponsoring the monastic community, and building, according to legend, 84,000 stupas (funerary monuments). He's honored by the Buddhist community as a paragon of Buddhist virtue, and his championing of the secular virtues of Buddhism sets the stage for the emergence of Mahayana Buddhism.

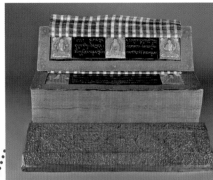

c. 247 B.C. According to Theravada tradition, Emperor Ashoka Maurya Sponsors a Third Buddhist Council at Pataliputra in India at which the famous commentary the *Kathavatthu* (*Points of Controversy*) is composed by monk Moggaliputta Tissa. It outlines the doctrinal differences between sects that eventually evolve into the split between Hinayana ("lesser vehicle") and Mahayana ("greater vehicle") Buddhism.

c. 230 B.C. Theravada Buddhism is officially introduced to Sri Lanka by the Venerable Mahinda, the son of Emperor Ashoka of India and 6 other monks during the reign of Devanampiya Tissa, who became the first Sri Lankan Buddhist king. Venerable Mahinda introduces the Buddhist canon to Sri Lanka.

200 B.C.

213 B.C. The great emperor Shih Huang-ti, first ruler to unify the warring provinces of China and founder of the short-lived Ch'in dynasty, institutes wide-ranging cultural reforms, including building the Great Wall, introducing a new currency, and replacing the old form of writing using a metal stylus with brush calligraphy on silk, resulting in the simplification of the Chinese character system. In response to resistance by Confucian traditionalists, the emperor orders a countrywide burning of books in this year, including Confucian and Taoist classics, with the aim of erasing all record of the past. It's said that 460 scholars were buried alive for treason. After the emperor's demise a few years later, revised versions of the classics are composed and much commentary added. Ironically, this ensures the longevity of the Confucian and Taoist traditions and ushers in a long tradition of textual criticism.

168–164 B.C. The Maccabeean Rebellion is waged against the occupation of Israel by ruler of the Seleucid Empire, Antiochus IV Epiphanes, who seizes control of the Jewish temple and, dedicating it to the Greek god Zeus, refuses to let Jews worship. Judas, son of priest Mattathias, recaptures Jerusalem and rededicates the Temple. He's given the name Maccabee ("hammer") as a title of honor. The festival of Hanukkah commemorates this event.

164 B.C. The Old Testament book of Daniel is finalized.

c. 150 B.C. Indo-Greek king Menander I converts to Buddhism under the influence of the sage Nagasena, according to the account of the *Milindapanha, Questions of Milinda (Menander)*, an influential text of Theravada Buddhism written in the 1st or 2nd century A.D. Menander's reign is long (c. 150–130 B.C.) and successful, and his coins bearing Buddhist symbols are found more widely than those of any other Indo-Greek king.

c. 150 B.C. Hinduism: The Yoga Sutras of Patanjali are composed. Regarded as the fundamental treatise on yoga (Sanskrit for "yoking" or "discipline"), one of the 6 orthodox systems of Indian philosophy, the text presents the 8-fold (*aṣṭāṅga*) path of yoga, which includes physical cleanliness and ethical restraint, physical postures (*āsana*), breath control, and mental disciplines of concentration aimed at freeing the yogi from the bondage of the senses and attaining liberation.

c. 100 B.C. The Pali version of the *Tripitaka*, the Buddhist canon, is compiled in Sri Lanka under the reign of King Vattagamani Abhaya.

63 B.C. Roman general Pompey comes to Israel to settle the dispute between Jewish parties of Sadducees and Pharisees. Israel becomes a Roman province.

47 B.C. Tradition holds that the Library of Alexandria in Egypt is burned by Romans under Julius Caesar, destroying priceless records of the wisdom of the ancient world. An alternate story records the destruction in 391.

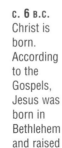

100 B.C.

68 B.C. Legend holds that Chinese Taoist and alchemist Li Shao-chün persuades the emperor Wu Ti that immortality can be achieved by eating from cinnabar vessels that had been transformed into gold. The first to claim that the goal of Taoism was to become an immortal master (*hsien*), he establishes physical and dietary regimens aimed toward this goal that becomes an established aspect of Taoist practice.

c. 6 B.C. Christ is born. According to the Gospels, Jesus was born in Bethlehem and raised

in the town of Nazareth in Galilee, the son of a carpenter, Joseph, and his wife, Mary. The Gospel of Mark (6:3) reports that he had at least 6 siblings.

Dating the Life of Christ

Dating the life of Jesus with historical accuracy is difficult, due to inconsistencies in the early texts. The first Gospel, Mark, was written around 65 A.D., several decades after the death of Jesus, and no independent records exist. However, working with chronological details mentioned in the Gospels, and comparing them to known historical events, many scholars place the approximate dates of Jesus' birth at between 8 B.C. and 6 A.D., near or during the reign of Herod the Great. A rough approximation of events of Jesus' life recorded in the Gospels is presented here.

Jesus' Childhood

Though little is known of Jesus' youth, the Gospel of Luke (2:41–52) records the story of Jesus as a 12-year-old boy who accompanies his parents to Passover in Jerusalem, staying behind for three days in the temple, engaging in religious discourse with learned teachers and astonishing all with the depth of his wisdom. When questioned by his parents, Jesus says, "Why did you seek Me? Did you not know that I must be about My Father's business?"

Baptism, Temptation, Ministry

The Gospel of Luke (3:21) reports that when Jesus is about 30 years old, he is baptized by John the Baptist, marking the start of his healing and teaching ministry. He is first, however, led by Spirit into the wilderness, where he experiences temptation by the Devil, fasting for 40 days. Emerging triumphant from this challenge, Jesus begins to travel to local synagogues, spreading the Good News.

Jesus' Message

In the course of his preaching, Jesus gathers a number of disciples, from which are chosen the Twelve Apostles. The Gospels portray Jesus performing many acts of healing and miracles, such as the raising of Lazarus from the dead (John 11:41–44), and turning loaves into fishes (Mark 8:5–9). The message of Jesus, often presented in parables, is characterized by an apocalyptic tone and a call to moral righteousness, demonstrated by brotherly love.

Passion

The Gospel accounts indicate that Jesus' ministry lasts between 1 and 3 years, and culminates with Jesus' attendance of Passover at Jerusalem, during which he shares the Last Supper with the apostles. Betrayed by Judas, he's arrested at the garden of Gethsemane; tried by Jewish authorities; and then turned over to Pontius Pilate, condemned, flogged, and mocked; forced to wear a crown of thorns and purple robe; made to carry his cross to Golgotha; and crucified above a plaque reading "Jesus of Nazareth, King of the Jews." His last words are: "My God, My God, why have You forsaken Me?" (Mark 15:34)

Resurrection

Though they differ in details, the Gospels report that after Jesus' death, he makes extraordinary appearances to his followers beginning on the 3rd day. Though the exact nature of Christ's risen body is unclear, the Gospel of Luke portrays Christ eating a piece of fish and honeycomb (Luke 24:42). The appearance of Christ signifies his identity as the Messiah, and his immanent second coming. The Book of Acts of the Apostles reports that the disciples gather in Jerusalem, where on Pentecost, 50 days after Passover and the resurrection of Jesus, he once again appears to them with "a sound from heaven as of a rushing mighty wind . . . and there appeared to them divided tongues, as of fire, and one sat upon each of them" (Acts 2:2–3) filling each with the Holy Spirit. The apostles now begin to preach openly the message of the Gospels.

14 A.D. Death of Caesar Augustus, 1st Emperor of Rome from 31 B.C.–14 A.D., and instigator of the nearly 200-year period of *Pax Romana* or "Roman peace," a time of peace and stability in the empire. He is deified upon his death, undergoing the

process of apotheosis, whereby he is officially declared a god. The ceremony involves a wax image of the emperor which is ritually burnt, and an eagle released to carry the soul to the gods. The apotheosis of Caesar Augustus begins the cult of the divine emperor during the Roman Empire.

10 A.D.

14–37 A.D. Reign of Tiberius, Roman emperor who suppresses the Druids. Most of what is known about the Druids comes from Roman sources that describe them as the learned class of Celtic culture. Druid

youths join the sacred order, and study poetry, astronomy, natural science, and sacred lore for up to 20 years before serving as teachers, judges, or priests presiding over the sacrifices. The Druid order is headed by a chief, and each year the Druids gather in a sacred location for a conclave. Druid power wanes with the coming of the Romans and with Christianity, but lives on in the rich tradition of oral lore.

C. 50 A.D. The beginning of the Christian church in the Roman Empire dates from this period, with the missionary activity of the Apostle Paul who devotes much of his career to founding churches in the cities of the Mediterranean. New Testament writings begin with the Pauline Epistles, including 1 and 2 Corinthians, Philippians, and Philemon. These letters contain encouragement and advice to the struggling new Christian communities. In all, 13 letters are attributed to Paul, though scholars debate the authenticity of several.

Celtic Religion in Gaul and Ireland

Since Celtic tradition was oral, no writing survives to tell us of the Celts' religious practices. We do know, however, that they buried their dead with food and personal items, indicating a belief in the afterlife and possibly reincarnation. Stories have survived that reveal a strong shamanic element, with many tales of humans transforming into animals, and a reverence for the natural world. Their most honored god was Lugus, patron of the arts, along with Cernunnos, horned god of the animals, and several goddesses, known by various names such as Epona, goddess of mares, and Morrigan, the crow goddess. Many animals had spiritual importance, such as the raven, the stag, and the bull. The natural landscape was understood to be full of spirits, especially in such places as springs and groves, and much of the traditional fairy faith of later days can be traced to Celtic origins. Yearly festivals marked the turning of the seasons, like the Irish spring festival of Beltane. The Celts apparently practiced human sacrifice, often of criminals, building large wicker frames and placing multiple victims inside.

The Apostle Paul: Second Founder of Christianity

After Jesus himself, no one has had more influence on the fate of Christianity than the Apostle Paul, who is largely responsible for spreading the faith to the pagan world of Rome. Paul was born Saul of Tarsus, a Jew and Roman citizen who was, in his younger life, a strict Pharisee, known for his piety in observance of the Mosaic Law dedicated to persecuting Christians. His conversion experience happens on the road to Damascus, where he's overcome by a blinding light, hearing the voice of Jesus saying, "Saul, Saul, why are you persecuting me?" He's blinded for 3 days and led by the hand to Damascus, where he begins his preaching ministry (Acts 9:3–8). Paul spends the remainder of his life developing Christian churches, and traveling to Antioch, Cyprus, and many places around the Mediterranean.

66 A.D. After years of growing discontent under brutal and repressive Roman rule, revolt breaks out among the Jews and is met by Roman retaliation, first under Vespasian, then his son, Titus.

65 A.D. Tradition records that Emperor Ming Ti of the Later Han dynasty in China allows a statue of the Buddha to be erected and the Buddhist message to be spread for the first time. It's said that the emperor became interested in Buddhism because of a dream in which the image of a flying golden Buddha appears to him in his chambers. Inspired by this vision, he sends 12 envoys to India to bring back knowledge of the foreign faith; they return with scriptures, statues, and two Buddhist monks. Residing in the monastery the emperor built for them, the monks teach Buddhism and translate the first Buddhist scriptures into Chinese, such as the Diamond Sutra and the Heart Sutra, Mahayana texts.

68 A.D. Although no definitive archaeological evidence exists, the most commonly held theory states that Roman legions under Vespasian destroy the Dead Sea Qumran community during the Second Jewish Revolt of A.D. 66–70. This site, where the Dead Sea Scrolls were found in 1947, might have been the location of a Jewish spiritual community that some scholars identify as the Essenes, a sect that split from the mainstream Jewish community in the 2nd century B.C. when the Maccabees took over the high priesthood of the Jerusalem Temple. Known for their pious observance of the Jewish law, simple communal lifestyle, and healing abilities, the Essenes had opposed Maccabeean rule and were in turn persecuted and forced to flee to the wilderness.

The siege lasts for years, driving Jewish resisters into an ever-narrowing area, finally within the Temple precincts, starving and wounded but refusing to surrender. In 70 A.D., the Roman forces breach the walls of the Temple and set it ablaze, razing the city in a bloody slaughter in which countless Jews are killed. This marks the end of the Second Temple and the period of Jewish national autonomy. The great Diaspora follows, and Jews leave the Holy Land for Babylonia, Arabia, Syria, and the far reaches of the Mediterranean world. A few remain in rural Palestine, still harboring revolutionary hopes that will erupt 60 years later.

C. 70 A.D. New Testament Gospel of Mark is written. The shortest and probably the first of the four canonical Gospels, the apocalyptic tone of the text probably represents oral tradition among the budding Christian community in the wake of the destruction of the Temple of Jerusalem. Mark tells of the preaching and miracles of Jesus, foretells the destruction of the Temple, and contains the

passion narrative of the crucifixion and resurrection, but does not contain the story of Jesus' birth. The original version ends with the discovery of Jesus' empty tomb by his female disciples; it's given a more affirmative ending by later redactors. The later Gospel of Matthew and Gospel of Luke incorporate the material of Mark, therefore these three are known as the "synoptic" Gospels.

C. 80 A.D. Revelation of St. John, final book of the New Testament, is composed. An apocalyptic text, the Revelation features mystical symbolic visions that indicate the impending end of the world and the following thousand-year reign of Christ. The text probably reflects the historical tensions of the early Christians under Roman persecution.

C. 85 A.D. New Testament Gospel of Luke and the Book of Acts are written by the same author as part of a 2-volume work written in polished literary Greek to appeal to the Gentile community. Along with Mark and Matthew, Luke completes the synoptic Gospels. Luke tells of Jesus' birth, preaching, and passion, and focuses on the message of Jesus as savior. The

Book of Acts tells the story of the formation of the early Christian church and follows the missionary activity of apostle Paul in his journey from Jerusalem to Rome, ending there with his imprisonment and triumphant preaching of the Word.

C. 85 A.D. New Testament Gospel of Matthew is written. Matthew adds the story of the birth of Jesus to his account, beginning with a genealogy that links Jesus to the lineage of Abraham, thereby emphasizing his link to Jewish tradition. Scholars generally agree that the text was written at Antioch in Syria sometime after the destruction of Jerusalem. The text reflects the atmosphere of social tension surrounding the early Christian movement, as it portrays the hostility between Jesus' followers and Jewish groups such as the Pharisees.

Authorship of the Gospels

The Gospels (from the Greek *euangelion,* "good news") are a unique genre of Christian text, telling stories about Jesus' life and deeds, his sayings, and the narrative of his death and resurrection. Each of the four Gospels, however, differs in language, style, and theological orientations. Key developments in modern biblical scholarship have come from analysis of the Gospels, examining them for clues about when and where they were written and the particular social and political struggles they reflect. In fact, their authorship is not known, and the traditional ascriptions (Mark, etc.) are an early tradition of the Church.

A striking variety of perspectives is revealed in the Gospels. For example in Mark and Matthew we find the followers of Jesus identifying themselves as a Jewish sect and observing the Mosaic Law, yet in Luke we find a greater orientation toward the cosmopolitan Greek world. Mark contains no account of Jesus' birth; this is added and developed in the successive Gospels. The progression is complete with the mystical Gospel of John, which transposes the story of Jesus to a spiritual and symbolic level that combines Jewish and Greek elements.

C. 90 A.D. New Testament Gospel of John is written. The last of the four canonical Gospels, John takes a mystical and revelatory tone that distinguishes it from the previous three Gospels, presenting Jesus as the Word of God incarnate. Scholarly evidence suggests that the text may reflect a combination of Jewish and Greek mystical ideas related to the Qumran Dead Sea community of the late 1st century, such as the struggle between light and darkness.

C. 90 A.D. The 24 books of the Hebrew Old Testament (Tanakh) are canonized in their final version. In 69 A.D. in the wake of the Diaspora following the destruction of Jerusalem, a group of rabbis escaped to the coastal town of Jabneh (Jamnia) where an academy was founded by Rabbi Johanan ben Zakkai, a follower of the famous Rabbi Hillel. Their goal is to preserve Jewish tradition by systematizing and recording its laws and teachings. The final selection of the biblical books, in particular the contents of the Ketuvim ("writings") are added to the existing Hebrew canon, and the excluded texts, such as Tobit, Judith, and the Wisdom of Solomon, are considered apocrypha ("hidden").

C. 100 A.D. Likely the earliest date of composition of the Nag Hammadi Scriptures, commonly known as the Gnostic Gospels, named for their discovery at the town of Nag Hammadi, Egypt, in 1945. The most complete existing collection of Gnostic manuscripts, the collection consists of 12 bound papyrus codices plus fragments of a 13th text, totaling over 1,000 pages. Encompasses a wide range of literature including Greek wisdom texts and Christian Gnostic texts in Coptic Egyptian translated from earlier Greek originals, among them the famous Gospel of Thomas, Gospel of Truth, and the Apocalypse of Paul. The Gnostic texts differ substantially from the canonical New Testament, often containing alternate traditions about Jesus and his teachings that point to a personal, mystic realization of truth.

100 A.D.

35

Gnosticism

From the Greek *gnosis* ("knowledge") the term Gnosticism is used to denote a number of Christian groups in the 2nd and 3rd centuries A.D. denounced by Church fathers as heretical to accepted Church doctrine. More recently, the term has been used for a number of religions of the ancient world that share key characteristics: Thus there are Jewish, Islamic, and Greek Gnostic texts as well. Gnostic teaching is typified by a dualistic view that holds light, truth, and goodness, identified with spirit, against darkness and falsehood, identified with the body and the physical world. The Gnostics apparently cultivated an ascetic approach that focused on denying the body and material world and striving for the return of the imprisoned spirit to its true home in the realm of light. Gnostic texts emphasize realization through individual mystic revelation (gnosis), rather than through the intermediaries of priests and sacraments of the organized church.

132–135 Simeon bar Kochba leads an unsuccessful revolt against the Romans occupying Palestine. Messianic sentiments had simmered among the Jewish people since the destruction of Jerusalem and in 131 Emperor Hadrian attempted to impose Roman customs, erecting a temple to Jupiter on the ruins of the Jerusalem temple. Bar Kochba leads the resistance and is hailed as a Messianic figure descended from the lineage of David. Jewish

forces seem victorious for a time, but with Roman reinforcements of about 35,000 men, Jerusalem is eventually recaptured and bar Kochba is killed. Jewish casualties number in the hundreds of thousands, and Jerusalem is thenceforth prohibited to Jews. The failure of the revolt effectively ends Jewish hopes for the imminent return of the Messiah and the restoration of the homeland.

142 Founding of Five Bushels of Rice Way or "Way of the Celestial Masters," a popular Taoist movement that threatens the government of the ruling Han dynasty. (Each household pays a tax of five bushels of

rice, thus giving rise to the popular name of the movement.) Ritual practices focus on healing through the invocation of spirits by officiating priests. Designated "Celestial Master" Chang Lu later forms an army and rebel theocratic state with the support of the impoverished peasant populace. In 215, after an internal schism, Chang Lu surrenders to the Han authorities.

148 An Shi-kao, a Parthian prince and Buddhist monk who renounced his throne to spread the Buddha's word, arrives in China at the Han dynasty capital of Loyang and makes the first translations of Theravada texts into Chinese. In 181 he's joined by a fellow Parthian monk, An Hsuan, who translates Mahayana texts.

150

150 Traditional date of the composition of the *Sepher ha Zohar* (*Book of Splendor*), a key text of Kabbalah mysticism, attributed to Simeon bar Yohai, a 2nd-century rabbi who helps revive Jewish scholarship after the Bar Kochba revolt. The *Zohar* lays forth a mystical interpretation of Biblical texts and presents the scheme of the 10 divine emanations or *sephirot* of creation. Historical scholarship holds that the *Zohar* in its present form was largely the work of 13th-century mystic Moses de León, and widespread popularity of the text occurred at that time.

Kabbalah Mysticism

Kabbalah ("reception") is the most influential form of Jewish mysticism and is an esoteric system for understanding and practicing the teachings and laws of the Torah. Central to Kabbalistic practice is the idea of man's participation in or "repair" of creation (*tikkun olam*), which in some systems was thought to have been originally flawed. The mechanism of creation is the 10 *sephirot* ("numbers"), spheres of divine emanation from the godhead or infinite (*"ein soph"*) moving toward increasingly dense levels of creation: *Keter* (crown), *Hokhhama* (wisdom), *Binah* (understanding), *Chesed* (mercy), *Gevurah* (power), *Tiferet* (beauty), *Netsach* (longevity), *Hod* (majesty), *Yesod* (foundation), and *Malkhut* (kingdom). The *sephirot* are combined in various ways, often arranged into a scheme of three pillars, representing the masculine, feminine, and mixed principles. The Kabbalist strives to bring about balance and harmony among these forces through his actions.

c. 150–250 Life of Nagarjuna, Indian monk-philosopher and founder of the Madhyamika school of Mahayana Buddhism, which teaches the doctrine of "emptiness" (*sūnyatā)* that all phenomena are empty of intrinsic nature and exist as pure relativity. Nagarjuna, born a Brahmin, converts to Buddhism and achieves great prowess as a teacher and debater, writing many philosophical treatises. Legend also holds that he's an accomplished tantric yogi, though scholars doubt the historical accuracy of this.

178 The Kushan monk Lokaksema resides in the court of the Han dynasty in China and translates important Mayayana texts until 189. Born in Gandhara during the rule of King Kanishka who sponsored the Fourth Buddhist Council, Lokaksema travels to China to spread the Buddhist teachings. There he introduces the Pure Land scriptures, which feature the heavenly realm of Buddha Amitabha and the Perfection of Wisdom Sutra (*Prajñāpāramitā Sūtra*), a seminal text of Mahayana Buddhism.

184 The Yellow Turban movement in China revolts against the Han dynasty, contributing to its fall in 220 A.D. The Taoist group is led by a charismatic mystic and healer, Chang Chüeh, who draws many faithful followers during a time of plague. The group is named for the yellow head coverings they wear. The rebellion lasts for 2 decades, until c. 204.

c. 200 The earlier Mahayana Buddhist scriptures are written about this time in India. Includes the Lotus Sutra, which teaches that the Buddha is eternally enlightened and all beings may enter into Buddhahood through the grace of faith, and the Buddhacharita of Ashvagosha, a spiritual biography of the Buddha in the high literary tradition of Sanskrit that enjoys great popularity.

c. 220 The Mishnah commentary on the Torah is finalized, marking an important stage in the development of rabbinic Judaism. Rabbinic schools in Galilee in the tradition of Rabbi Akiba classify the unwritten tradition of Torah commentary under 6 headings—including Agriculture, Holy Things, and Purity—and create a veritable encyclopedia of 4,000 precepts of law of the great rabbis of past generations. Over time the Mishnah acquires a status second only to the Torah itself.

200

Mayan Classical Phase: c. 250–900

Maya culture shares much with the earlier Olmec culture. Maya mythology centers around the creator god Itzamná, the feathered serpent Kukulcán, and gods of corn, rain, and other natural phenomena. A priesthood presides over religious rites, which include ritual human sacrifice, self-mutilation, and rites to escort the dead through the underworld. Much attention is paid to the royal dead, thought to be descended from gods, with great pyramids built as tombs for them, dating from as early as 300 B.C. The Mayan 260-day sacred calendar (*tzolkin*) forms the basis of a complex ritual cycle, used as a tool for divination, determining the good and evil influences for each day. The "Great Cycle"—and history itself, some assert—which began in 3114 B.C., reaches an end after 1,872,000 days, which will occur in the year 2012.

c. 274 Mani, Iranian founder of Manichaeism, dies. Mani is regarded as the last prophet in a lineage including Adam, Buddha, Zoroaster, and Jesus. His religion enjoyed considerable popularity, spreading to Egypt, North Africa, and Rome in the 4th century where it was attacked by the Christian church as a heresy. It spreads as far as China and East Turkestan in the 7th and 8th centuries, and persists in Persia until the 10th century.

300

325 The Council of Nicea, the First Ecumenical Council of the Christian church, is convened by Emperor Constantine I after coming to power in 324 as sole ruler of the entire Roman empire.

About 300 bishops meet to discuss theological questions about the nature of Christ that are not yet defined.

313 Constantine I, the first Roman emperor to become a Christian, issues the Edict of Milan granting religious tolerance to Christians. In 312 Constantine becomes emperor of the Western Roman empire after a series of military victories. Legend has it that in his rise to power, Constantine had a vision on the battlefield of the Holy Cross in the heavens with the words "In this sign you shall conquer" (*in hoc signo vinces*), spurring his conversion.

Manichaeism

Manichaeism is a gnostic dualistic religion of Persia that regards the world as a mixture of good and evil principles—the fallen spirit must transcend the ignorance of matter and recover its true spiritual nature. The religion was widespread in its day. The great 4th-century Christian theologian Saint Augustine of Hippo was Manichaean in his early life, and the religion may have influenced a number of European sects of the Middle Ages, such as the Bogomils of 10th-century Bulgaria and the Cathari, or Albigensians, of 12th-century France.

330 Emperor Constantine dedicates St. Peter's Basilica, located on the traditional burial site of St. Peter in Rome on Vatican Hill.

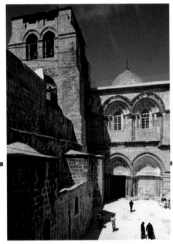

336 Emperor Constantine dedicates the Church of the Holy Sepulchre in Jerusalem (seen above) on the traditional site of Jesus Christ's crucifixion and burial. The church has been destroyed and rebuilt numerous times over the centuries, and remains an important holy site today.

350 The Avesta is restored by Sassanian kings in the language of Pahlavi after it was destroyed by Alexander the Great when he conquered Persia. The text is

the primary scripture of Zoroastrianism and contains hymns, or *gathas*, instructions for the *yasna*, the Zoroastrian liturgical rituals, as well as mythological accounts of creation.

381 Council of Constantinople, Second Ecumenical Council of the Christian church, is convened by Emperor Theodosius I. It expands the Nicene Creed and definitively formulates the doctrine of the Holy Trinity, declaring equality among all three members, Father, Son, and Holy Spirit. In 383, the emperor declares Christianity the imperial state religion of Rome.

Arius and the Nicene Creed

One of the doctrines debated by the Council of Nicea is that of the learned Alexandrian Arius who holds that Christ must be created, as are all creatures, and can not be of the same nature or substance as God. This doctrine comes to be called Arianism and greatly influences early Christians, threatening to tear the church apart. In response, the bishops at Nicea produce a statement of doctrine, known as the Nicene Creed, which proclaims that Jesus Christ, the Son, was "of one substance (*homoousios*) with the Father," thereby condemning Arianism as a heresy. Arius is exiled by the emperor.

391 Christian Emperor Theodosius I issues decrees outlawing pagan worship and shortly thereafter orders the destruction of pagan temples, including the famous Serapeum, the temple to the god Serapis in Alexandria. The pagan temples dedicated to the Mystery religions are desecrated.

c. 398 St. Augustine of Hippo, influential bishop and theologian, writes his *Confessions*, telling the story of his youth and conversion to Christianity. Augustine is born pagan in North Africa and follows the dualistic Manichean religion for years until he meets his mentor, Bishop Ambrose, and has a mystical conversion experience. In 387 he's baptized, and in 396 becomes bishop of Hippo Regius. He writes prolifically and his ideas on predestination and the nature of sin greatly influence later Christian thinkers. Among his best-known works are *The City of God*, *On Christian Doctrine*, and *On the Trinity*.

396 The cult of the Eleusianian Mysteries definitively ends as Alaric the Goth invades Greece accompanied by Christians, destroying and desecrating the sacred sites. The sites had been in decline for some time due to the rise of Christianity as the state religion of Rome.

400 The earliest Puranas ("ancient lore")—collections of popular Hindu traditions—are composed. This genre of sacred Hindu literature is the source of much of the classic mythology of Hinduism, including stories of the gods Vishnu, Shiva, and Brahma, as well as many others. Myths of creation, including a vast cosmology of *yugas*—cycles of creation and destruction of the cosmos—are portrayed, as well as the royal lineage of kings. The most popular is the Bhagavata Purana, which portrays the life of the god Krishna. The composition of Puranas continues until c. 1000.

c. 400 Life of St. Patrick, patron saint of Ireland, traditionally credited with bringing the Christian faith to that land. He's a legendary figure in Irish folklore, known for driving the serpents out of that land, and the shamrock, symbol of the trinity, is associated with him. His feast is celebrated on March 17, traditionally the day of his death.

St. Patrick

The story of St. Patrick begins with him being born in Britain and then being captured as a youth and enslaved in Ireland under a Druid priest. After some years there he has a vision inspiring him to escape. He flees Ireland and becomes a monk, but some years later, hears voices foretelling his return to that northern land. He endures great hardship bringing the Christian message to Ireland, eventually gaining many followers among the Picts and Anglo-Saxons and establishing the faith.

c. 400 The Palestinian Talmud is composed, a collection of rabbinic commentary on the Mishnah and oral law by the descendants of the rabbinic schools that had produced the Mishnah. There are two independent Talmuds, the other being the more extensive Babylonian version compiled c. 600. Both are organized in a similar format, containing commentary and analysis of selected Torah passages.

c. 400 Composition of the Mahabharata ("Great story of the Bharatas"), one of the two great Hindu epics (the other being the *Ramayana*). In its final form, it's almost 100,000 verses long and tells of the heroic battle between two groups of cousins, the Kauravas and the Pandavas, for possession of the throne, traditionally regarded as the forebears of Indian Hindus. The epic explores the notion of dharma or proper moral conduct as it pertains to roles such as kingship and asceticism. The Mahabharata contains within it the scripture the Bhagavad Gita ("Song of the Lord"), one of the most popular devotional works of Hinduism which focuses on worship of the divine incarnation of the god Krishna.

401 At the request of the Chinese emperor, Kuchean monk Kumarajiva is brought to the capital Ch'ang-an and translates many Sanskrit Buddhist texts into Chinese, including the Heart Sutra and other important Mahayana texts. He heads a famous school of translators sponsored by the emperor and is influential in spreading Buddhist teachings in China.

402 Chinese Buddhist monk Fa-hsien makes an overland pilgrimage from China to India, to visit Buddhist holy sites and bring back scriptures. After studying in India for 10 years, he returns to China to translate Buddhist scriptures from Sanskrit into Chinese, returning by sea and spending 2 years in Sri Lanka along the way. His diaries provide an invaluable record of the flourishing Buddhist culture of India during that time.

405 The Vulgate (Latin Bible) is codified by St. Jerome from Greek and Hebrew versions. The project, commissioned by Pope Damasus in 382, is produced in several stages. Though Jerome's version doesn't immediately enjoy universal acceptance, it gradually gains favor, and in 1546 the Roman Catholic Church will proclaim it the authoritative Latin source.

440 Consecration of Pope Leo I, sometimes referred to as the "first Pope." During his Papacy, he argues for greater influence for the office of Pope, proclaiming that papal power was granted by Christ to St. Peter and could only be passed to his successors, the bishops of Rome. He exercises great political influence as well, and at a time when the Roman Empire is crumbling, convinces Attila the Hun not to attack Rome in 452 and helps to soften the impact of Vandal occupation of the city in 455. He holds office until 461.

476 The Germanic chieftain Odovacar deposes the last Emperor Romulus Augustus and the Imperial Insignia is sent to Constantinople, marking the end of the Western Roman Empire. The Byzantine Empire in the East continues.

500

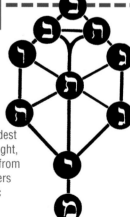

451 The Fourth Ecumenical Council of the Christian church takes place at Chalcedon in Asia Minor. The doctrine of the trinity continues to be refined, and differences between Western and Eastern churches emerge on the question of how the divine and human aspects of Christ coexist. The council codifies a comprehensive statement of the trinity that incorporates the earlier Nicene and Constantinople creeds and becomes standard Catholic doctrine. This Council, the largest recorded, was attended by over 500 bishops.

c. 500 The Sepher Yetzirah (Book of Creation) is composed. Perhaps the oldest known treatise on Jewish magical thought, it claims that the cosmos was created from 22 divine Hebrew letters and 10 numbers or *sephirot*, the basis of the Kabbalistic tradition.

520 Ch'an (Zen) Buddhism is brought to China by Indian monk Bodhidharma. A native of Southern India, tradition records that he travels to China where he meets with emperor Wu Ti of the Southern Liang dynasty, known

for his pious acts. The emperor asks Bodhidharma what benefits he might receive as a result of his good acts, to which Bodhidharma reputedly replies that good works contain no merit whatsoever. The monk is then dismissed from the emperor's company and sits in meditation with his face to a wall for 9 years.

Ch'an/Zen Buddhism

Zen Buddhism is the Japanese translation of the Chinese term *ch'an*, which in turn is a translation of the Sanskrit *dhyana* meaning "meditation." Thus, Zen Buddhism is the "meditation school," a direct approach to enlightenment that emphasizes meditation rather than study of scriptures. Though the root doctrines originated in India, Zen evolves into a distinctive school first in China, as Ch'an, brought by the patriarch Bodhidharma, and then takes root in Japan beginning in the 12th century. Zen holds that sudden awakening to one's Buddha nature is possible. It comes to be heavily influenced by Taoist ideas and in many ways differs in tone from the classical Indian Buddhist traditions which tend to emphasize study of the scriptures, analytic examination of self and phenomena, and a gradual path to enlightenment combining insight and cultivation of virtue.

552 Buddhism reaches Japan from Korea, a gift from the King of Paekche who is hoping for military assistance to fight off his enemies. He sends Japanese Emperor Kimmei a gold Buddha image and Buddhist texts claiming the magical power of the Buddhist doctrine. After much discussion in the Japanese court as

to whether the new religion would displease the local *kami* or deities, the gift is tentatively accepted; however, when a plague breaks out, the Buddha image is thrown into a ditch. After several such offerings, the new religion is finally accepted and begins to enjoy increasing favor among the royal court for its philosophical breadth and the social-mindedness of Mahayana teachings of compassion toward all creatures.

563 Irish monk and missionary St. Columba goes to Scotland and founds a Christian monastery on the Isle of Iona. His monastery is the only center for study in the region, and the learned Columba is respected as a man of diplomacy among the feuding Pict tribes whom he works to convert. Many miracles surround his life: The first known reference to the Loch Ness Monster occurs in a story of how he turns back the beast from devouring a swimmer by making the sign of the cross.

Islam

Islam, from the Arabic meaning "to submit [to the will of *Allāh*]," is, after Judaism and Christianity, the third of the monotheistic faiths based on the lineage of Abraham. Islam brings the revelation of God (Arabic, *Allāh*)—regarded as the same God of the Old and New Testaments—to the Arab people with a scripture of their own, the Koran. Muhammad is believed to be the final prophet in a lineage including Adam, Abraham, Moses, and Jesus, and is known as the "seal of the prophets." The Koran is regarded as God's only miracle, an earthly replica of the "heavenly book" of living revelation. The main duties of an observant Muslim are contained in the Five Pillars: *shahāda*, or profession of faith; *salāt* or ritual prayer five times per day; *zakāt*, alms tax for the poor and disadvantaged; *sawm*, fasting during the holy month of Ramadan; and *hajj*, the pilgrimage to Mecca that every able Muslim should perform at least once. Muhammad's role as a social reformer is unparalleled; he introduces Arab society to the practice of welfare for widows and orphans and gives women legal rights in marriage, divorce, and ownership of property. Two major sects of Islam develop, differing in their views of the succession of leadership after Muhammad: The Sunni majority of Muslims hold that the caliph is elected leader, and the Shi'ite minority hold that the imam, a descendant of Muhammad's son-in-law Ali is the rightful ruler. Holding the ideal of unity among the political, social, and religious spheres, Islam becomes a unifying force of Arab culture and beyond, reaching its peak as a world power in the 16th century with the Ottoman, Mughul, and Safavid dynasties.

c. 570–632 Life of Muhammad, Prophet of Allah and founder of Islam. Tradition records that Muhammad is born in Mecca, a thriving trade and pilgrimage center. He's raised by his mother, his father having died before his birth, until she dies too and he comes under the care of his uncle, Abu Talib. Muhammad's wife, Khadija, bears him two sons (both of whom he outlives), and four daughters. In 610 he's on retreat in the mountains when he has his first revelation: The angel Gabriel grips him and tells him to "recite" the first verses of the

Koran. Over the next few years, Muhammad begins preaching publicly and meets with modest success, as well as growing displeasure by the wealthy Meccans who feel that he's critical of their sometimes licentious ways. He eventually flees with his followers to the city of Medina, where he establishes the faith. After recapturing Mecca in 630, Muhammad dies unexpectedly of an illness in 632, without appointing a successor.

600

c. 600 The Babylonian Talmud, (the second Talmud along with the Palestinian Talmud) is compiled by the rabbinic community in exile in Babylon, the leading center of Jewish learning of the day. The Talmud, a vast repository of Jewish wisdom on the Torah, includes the Mishnah and the Gemara, rabbinic commentary on the Mishnah. Of the two, the Babylonian Talmud is more extensive, and has great scriptural authority.

610 The first revelations of the Koran are received by Muhammad through the angel Gabriel.

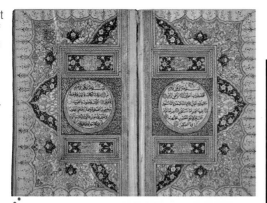

c. 627 Buddhism is established in Tibet. King Songtsen Gampo, who established Tibet as a great military power, marries two queens, one Nepalese and one Chinese, who each bring statues of Buddha that the king has installed in temples. One of those temples, the Jokhang, becomes the most sacred shrine in Tibet. As Tibet has no written language, the king sends scholar Thonmi Sambhota to Kashmir to study Sanskrit and devise a Tibetan script in order to translate the Buddhist scriptures into the native tongue.

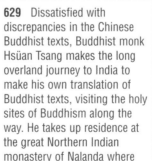

622 Muhammad and early followers undertake the *hijra*, or migration, fleeing from persecution in Mecca to Medina. There he establishes a center for his new religion, and, in a series of military campaigns, defeats the Meccan army. In 630 Muhammad rides triumphantly back into Mecca and rededicates the central shrine of the Ka'ba to Allah thus establishing it as the spiritual center of the Islamic world. The Muslim calendar begins from this time.

629 Dissatisfied with discrepancies in the Chinese Buddhist texts, Buddhist monk Hsüan Tsang makes the long overland journey to India to make his own translation of Buddhist texts, visiting the holy sites of Buddhism along the way. He takes up residence at the great Northern Indian monastery of Nalanda where he studies Sanskrit and Buddhist philosophy. There he gains the patronage of the king, who sponsors his journey back to China in 643 with many manuscripts. He devotes the remainder of his life to translating those manuscripts and establishes the Consciousness Only school of Buddhism. The cave of buddhas and bodhisattvas in China date from the time of the pilgrim Hsüan Tsang.

634 Umar ibn al-Khattab becomes the 2nd Caliph of Islam. Under his leadership, the Syrian city of Damascus is captured from Christian forces in 635 after a 6-month siege. In 638 the Muslim army conquers Jerusalem. In 642 the library of Alexandria in Egypt is destroyed for the third and final time by Muslim forces.

632 Muhammad dies and Abu Bakr is elected the first Caliph, religious and civil leader of Islam. He unites the Arab forces into an army of 10,000 and leads their conquest of Syria.

644 Uthman ibn Affan, son-in-law of Muhammad, is elected the third Caliph. Under his leadership from 644–656, Muslims conquer Cyprus and Tripoli and establish Islamic rule in Iran, Afghanistan, and Sind. He's later assassinated by dissenting Muslim factions.

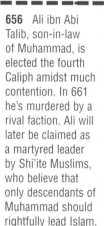

c. 650 The Koran is finalized during the reign of Uthman. Tradition holds that verses were written down during the Prophet Muhammad's lifetime, but are not compiled in an authoritative text until this time. The Koran consists of 114 verses, or *sūras*, each representing one or more revelations from the Prophet.

661 The Ummayad dynasty is founded under Caliph Muawiyyah I. The capital is moved from Medina to Damascus. Muslim territory extends from India to Spain.

656 Ali ibn Abi Talib, son-in-law of Muhammad, is elected the fourth Caliph amidst much contention. In 661 he's murdered by a rival faction. Ali will later be claimed as a martyred leader by Shi'ite Muslims, who believe that only descendants of Muhammad should rightfully lead Islam.

691 The Dome of the Rock, oldest standing Muslim monument, is completed in Jerusalem. Tradition holds that it stands on the spot where Muhammad tethered his steed Buraq before his ascent to heaven. It's regarded as the same place where Abraham offered his son as sacrifice as well as the site of Solomon's temple, making it a holy place for Muslims, Christians, and Jews alike.

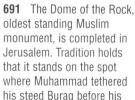

c. 700 The *Jataka* stories, popular tales of Buddha's previous lives, often as animals, are translated into Syriac and Arabic. The story of Buddha's life as Prince Siddhartha is translated into Greek by John of Damascus, and circulates to Christians as the

story of Barlaam and Josaphat. By the 1300s the story of Josaphat has become so popular that he's made a Catholic saint.

712 Shinto text, the Kojiki ("Records of Ancient Matters"), is written in Japan from long-standing oral tradition. Since Japan has no written language at the time, Chinese characters are used to represent Japanese sounds. The text contains myths and historical traditions that tell of the creation of Japan from the *kami*, or spirits, with sun goddess Amaterasu as the ancestor of the Japanese emperor.

700

720 The *Nihon Shoki* (*Chronicles of Japan*) is compiled from Japanese tradition. Along with the Kojiki, it comprises the oldest record of Japanese history, stretching from mythical beginnings to the 7th century. It's written in Chinese by order of the imperial court.

732 Charles Martel defeats an attack by Spanish Muslims at the

Battle of Tours in France and stops the Muslim advance into Europe.

Shinto

Shinto ("way of the *kami*") is Japan's native spiritual tradition. Centering around the worship of *kami*—which include spirits of nature, ancestors, deities, and the sacred essence in things—Shinto has no founder or official doctrine and represents the ancient traditions of the Japanese people. Though it has no official scriptures, the Kojiki and *Nihon Shoki* are regarded as the authoritative source of myth and tradition, but are written down only after Buddhism arrived in Japan. Shinto rituals often occur in connection with local shrines and are facilitated by priests. Festivals (*matsuri*) such as the spring festival (*haru matsuri*) are a central part of the Shinto tradition and are observed by the people, as well as in formal ceremonies by the emperor, who performs the function of ritually purifying the nation.

749 The Abbassid dynasty of Islam is established. In 762, Baghdad is made capital, and becomes renowned in the ancient world for its wealth and culture.

775 The first Buddhist monastery in Tibet, Samye, is founded by Buddhist tantric master Padmasambhava, founder of the Nyingmapa order.

c. 750 Composition of the *Tibetan Book of the Dead* (*Bardo Thödol*), a Buddhist manual that describes the landscape of the 49-day *bardo* or limbo of the dead before rebirth, including blissful and demonic appearances that entice and repel the wandering soul. Traditionally recited by a lama (Buddhist priest) at the deceased's side to guide the departed to a fortunate rebirth.

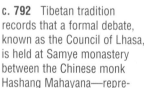

c. 792 Tibetan tradition records that a formal debate, known as the Council of Lhasa, is held at Samye monastery between the Chinese monk Hashang Mahayana—representing the Ch'an "sudden enlightenment" school that holds that "no thinking" leads to enlightenment—and the Indian monk Kamalashila—representing the "gradual" school of Indian Mahayana Buddhism that holds that moral and meditative cultivation is necessary. Both Chinese and Indian schools are influential in Tibet but the debate is reportedly won by Kamalashila, and the Indian gradual school is adopted henceforth as the Tibetan tradition. Tradition records that the Chinese monk committed suicide after his defeat.

c. 800 Written version of the Bundahishn ("Original Creation") is composed in Pahlavi. Containing mythological accounts of creation, the history of the world, and the origin of man, the Zoroastrian text is based on lost material from the Avesta, the primary scripture of Zoroastrianism, and preserves ancient Persian traditions.

838 Buddhists in Tibet are persecuted under King Lang Darma, a follower of the native Bön animistic tradition. He shuts down temples and monasteries, orders the destruction of Buddhist texts and images, and forces monks and nuns to disrobe, executing those who refuse. This marks the end of the period known as the "First Dissemination" of Buddhism.

804 Under the reign of Emperor Kammu of Japan, a fleet of 4 ships sail for China. Two ships make it, one carrying monk Kūkai, who studies the Vajrayana teachings and returns to Japan to found the Shingon tantric school of Buddhism. The other ship carries the monk Saichō, who returns to Japan to found the Tendai school, based on the Chinese Tiantai school centered on the teachings of the Lotus Sutra.

Persecution of Buddhism Under King Lang Darma

Buddhism is widespread in Tibet by the time King Lang Darma comes to power and continues in secret even while he persecutes its followers. One night while Lang Darma attends a dance performance, a Buddhist monk dresses in costume and dances before the king with a bow and arrow. Catching the king unaware, he shoots and kills him. After his death, Buddhism is once again adopted as the official religion of Tibet.

839 Al-Tabari, influential Muslim scholar, is born in Baghdad during the Abbassid dynasty. Journeying in his youth to study in Iraq, Syria, and Egypt, he collects the learned traditions of scholars all over the Muslim world, and compiles them into major works, the *Koran Commentary* and the *History of Prophets and Kings*.

c. 850 The great Buddhist monument Borobudur in Java, Indonesia, is completed after about 50 years of construction. Built in the pattern of a mandala—a symbolic depiction of the universe as a series of concentric circles within squares—the monument is filled with detailed carvings and statues depicting the stages of enlightenment, scenes from the life of the Buddha and Mahayana sutras, and culminates at the upper levels with images of celestial Buddhas representing the attainment of enlightenment. A few centuries after its construction the monument is buried after a volcanic eruption and abandoned until being restored in the 20th century by archaeologists and UNESCO.

841–846 Tang dynasty Emperor Wu-tsung launches a persecution of Buddhists at the height of Buddhist popularity in China, destroying almost 45,000 temples and shrines, tens of thousands of religious images, and defrocking over 250,000 monks and nuns. Buddhism never completely regains its former influence after this assault.

c. 868 The first printed Buddhist scriptures are produced in China, among them the Diamond Sutra.

c. 870 The *Hadith*, a collection of oral traditions about the life of Prophet Muhammad and his companions is compiled by Muslim scholar al-Bukhari. The hadith are an important source of religious law, or sunna ("right custom") in Islam, telling what the Prophet said and did in a variety of circumstances (the Koran itself has no reference to the life of Muhammad). During this period 6 major collections of *hadith* are established as canonical, but the collection of al-Bukhari is the most famous.

Sufism: Islamic Mysticism

Sufism is a mystical form of Islam that seeks direct personal experience of the love and wisdom of God (*Allah*). The Arabic word *"ṣūfī"* probably derives from the word "wool" (*ṣuf*), referring to the woolen clothing of early ascetics. Though Sufis trace their origins to the time of Muhammad, the movement gains recognition around the 8th century during the Umayyad dynasty. Sufis pursue divine union through practices such as reciting the names of God (*dhikr*, "remembering") and the whirling dance of the dervishes. Devotional poetry, in which the yearning for the divine is often likened to the desire for a lover, reaches an apex of literary achievement by Sufi mystics such as Rumi and Rabi'a.

900

922 Iraqi Sufi mystic and saint al-Hallaj is executed for blasphemy. Al-Hallaj is drawn to the mystical life from a young age and studies with some of the leading mystical teachers of the day, making several pilgrimages to Mecca and missionary journeys abroad. Although he attracts many disciples, his unorthodox views make him suspect in the eyes of the Abbassid authorities. The occasion for his arrest comes when, in a moment of spiritual ecstasy, he cries out "I am the Truth," taken as a blasphemous assertion of identity with *Allah*. After a long trial and imprisonment, al-Hallaj is crucified and tortured to death in front of a large crowd. The saint bears his ordeal calmly and forgives his torturers. He's regarded as a martyr by later Muslims.

932 The Engishiki, comprised of 50 sections, is composed during the Engi period of Japanese history. An information manual for Shinto rituals, it provides detailed instructions for carrying out ceremonies, including *norito*, or prayers, to be recited by priests.

980–1037 Life of Ibn Sina (Avicenna), the most famous philosopher and scientist of Islam, known for applying Greek philosophical thought to Islamic theology. A genius in his youth, he masters the fields of medicine, law, philosophy, and science. He gains patronage of Iranian rulers and becomes court physician and advisor, and devotes himself to scholarship and teaching. His works on medicine are translated into Latin in the 12th century and his theological works influence Medieval Christian theologians.

1000

1016–1100 Life of the Indian Buddhist Tantric master Naropa. He's a great scholar, according to tradition, and attains the post of abbot of the famous Nalanda Monastery in Northern India. A series of visions and events leads him to realize the limitations of his intellectual understanding and finally to meet his guru, Tilopa, who puts him through a series of tests lasting 12 years, including jumping from a tall building. Having at last purified his mind from false conceptions, Naropa is initiated into *mahāmudrā* the secret method of enlightenment, and he becomes fully realized. Naropa is regarded as a founder of the Kagyu school of Tibetan Buddhism.

1032–1107 Until 1107, the Ch'eng brothers, Ch'eng Hao and Ch'eng I, are leading figures in the formulation of Neo-Confucian philosophy in China. They develop their own philosophies, heavily influenced by Taoist and Buddhist ideas, and gather a large circle of disciples. Their ideas center on the notion of *li*, a metaphysical principle underlying all existence. While Ch'eng Hao emphasizes quietistic meditation, Ch'eng I stresses intellectual cultivation. Their ideas influence the great Neo-Confucian philosopher Chu Hsi a few years later.

c. 1039–c. 1123 Life of the Tibetan Tantric saint Milarepa, beloved folk hero of Tibetan Buddhism. He's famous for his songs of enlightenment and is regarded as a patriarch of the Kagyu lineage of Tibetan Buddhism.

Milarepa the Repentant Sorcerer

Legend records that Milarepa is forced into servitude as a young man after his family's property is stolen by relatives. His mother then urges him to learn black magic in order to enact revenge, but in a tragic turn, Milarepa accidentally kills a number of innocent people at a wedding, while his relatives escape unharmed. Feeling great remorse for the negative karma incurred by his deeds, Milarepa vows to pursue religion. He meets his guru Marpa, the "crazy yogi," who sets for him a series of daunting tasks, including building a stone tower, then tearing down and rebuilding it several times more, until he comes to the point of suicidal despair. Just as Milarepa's about to take his own life, Marpa proclaims that by his trials, Milarepa has purified his evil karma. He goes on to become a great enlightened yogi.

The Crusades

The Crusades are a series of military campaigns sanctioned by the Papacy that took place from the 11th to the 13th centuries. Though the original purpose was to recapture Jerusalem and the Holy Land from Muslim rule, some later Crusades reflect other agendas, such as the Albigensian Crusade aimed against the heretical sect by the same name. The Crusades frequently become mass movements, often expressing anti-Semitic hostilities, resulting in widespread massacres of Jews in Europe as well as the Holy Land. The Crusades have a great impact on Europe, paving the way for the emergence of the nation-state and the cultural developments of the Renaissance facilitated by increased trade and travel between Europe and the East.

1054 Eastern and Western Christian churches separate after centuries of growing discord. A Papal Legate excommunicates the patriarch of Constantinople, who responds by denouncing the Pope. The two branches of the Church remain separate to this day: Roman Catholicism with its seat in Rome, and the Eastern Orthodox Church with its seat in Constantinople.

1095 Answering an appeal from Byzantine Emperor Alexius I for assistance in fending off the Seljuk Turks, Pope Urban II preaches the First Crusade, promising penance for all who participate. After sacking several cities, the army of Crusaders conquers Jerusalem in 1099, resulting in a mass slaughter of the city's Jewish and Muslim inhabitants. Christian control of the city lasts until 1187 when it is recaptured by Muslim conqueror Saladin.

1111 Muslim philosopher and Sufi mystic al-Ghazali dies. He's most famous for his masterpiece, *The Revival of the Religious Sciences*, which makes Sufi mysticism compatible with the orthodox Sunni tradition. At a time when the Sunni establishment frowns upon Sufi mysticism, I-Ghazali demonstrates that the doctrines and observances of both traditions are compatible, which helps legitimate Sufi mysticism for coming generations of Muslims.

1100

1130–1200 Life of Chu Hsi, one of the most influential Neo-Confucian scholars in China. His own philosophy focuses on the metaphysical aspect of Confucian thought as a counter to the popular Buddhist and Taoist beliefs. He writes a number of scholarly works, including important commentaries on the Confucian classics, which, though considered heterodox during his life, are later adopted in the official Confucian curriculum. Some years after his death, his ancestral tablet is placed in the Confucian temple, a great honor.

1135–1204 Life of Moses Maimonides, a.k.a. "Rambam," the most influential Jewish philosopher of the medieval period. He's born to a prominent family in Cordoba, Spain, at a time when Jews are allowed to worship openly. Later relocating to Egypt in a time of persecution, Maimonides studies medicine, gaining great fame, and becomes the personal physician of Sultan Saladin, according to some accounts. Maimonides writes numerous philosophical and theological works of Torah commentary, his most famous being the *Mishne Torah*, a systematization of Jewish law that becomes the definitive work of its kind. He also authors the *Guide for the Perplexed*, which has become an enduring religious classic.

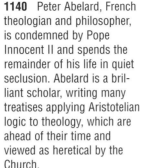

c. 1147 Hildegard of Bingen, German abbess and mystic, founds a new convent at Rupertsberg. Hildegard experiences visions from a young age and, while serving as a prioress in the cloister of Disibodenberg, receives a prophetic call instructing her to "write what you see." She hesitantly reports her visions to her confessor, and their authenticity is confirmed by a committee of theologians. She records her apocalyptic and prophetic visions in her work *Scivias*, written with the assistance of a Church-appointed scribe, and continues to write after founding the convent. Other works include treatises on medicine, natural history, and the lives of the saints. She's remembered today for her strikingly modern paintings (an illustration of hers, pictured) and evocative arrangements of devotional music.

1140 Peter Abelard, French theologian and philosopher, is condemned by Pope Innocent II and spends the remainder of his life in quiet seclusion. Abelard is a brilliant scholar, writing many treatises applying Aristotelian logic to theology, which are ahead of their time and viewed as heretical by the Church.

The Love Story of Abelard and Heloïse

A brilliant scholar in his youth, Abelard becomes a traveling teacher of Aristotelian logic. In Paris, he tutors the beautiful Heloïse, niece of Canon Fulbert, and the two have an affair. A child is born and they marry secretly, but when Canon Fulbert discovers them, he gets his revenge by having Abelard castrated. Abelard then becomes a monk at the royal abbey of Saint-Denis and forces Heloïse to become a nun. The two continue their love chastely, from afar. The letters between Abelard and Heloïse remain testimony to one of the most beloved medieval love stories.

1175 Hōnen, Buddhist monk and founder of Pure Land (*Jōdo*) Buddhism in Japan, proclaims that all that is needed for salvation is the *nembutsu*—recitation of the name of Amida Buddha. Taking monastic orders at the famous Mt. Hiei monastery, the young Hōnen is later disillusioned by the corruption there, and finds inspiration in the Pure Land doctrine of salvation through the mercy of Buddha. As his own school's popularity increases, he arouses the hostility of the Buddhist establishment, and is banished from the capital, Kyoto, in 1207. He continues his teaching in exile, and his school becomes one of the most influential in Japanese Buddhism.

1187 Saladin, Sultan of Egypt, defeats the Crusader kingdom in the Holy Land and returns Jerusalem to Muslim control. At the Battle of Hattin the Crusader army is decimated by Saladin and Crusader leader Raymond of Chatillon is captured and beheaded. Several months later the city is taken after 88 years of Crusader control. These events prompt the Third Crusade called by Pope Gregory VIII, but it doesn't succeed in reclaiming Jerusalem.

1198–1212 Reign of Pope Innocent III (Lothair of Segni). He presides over the Fourth Crusade (1202–04) and the Albigensian Crusade (1209–29). His reign marks the zenith of the Medieval papacy.

1191 Eisai founds the Rinzai school of Zen Buddhism in Japan. A Tendai monk, Eisai makes two trips from China to bring the pure Buddhist teaching to Japan. He establishes the Ch'an teachings of *zazen* meditation and contemplation of *koan*, or enigmatic statements, adding an emphasis on feudal practices such as the virtue of loyalty and developing martial arts of swordsmanship and archery, which wins great appeal with the samurai, or warrior class. Eisai founds several Rinzai monasteries and gains the patronage of the Shogun Minamoto Yoriie.

1198 Ibn Arabi, Islamic philosopher and mystic from Spain, has a vision to go on pilgrimage. Stopping first in Mecca (shown, black "veil" covering its holy shrine), he receives further divine inspiration to undertake his major work, *The Meccan Revelations*, an encyclopedic study of Muslim learning and personal insight. Falling in love with a beautiful maiden who becomes his muse, he begins to write mystical love poetry, collected in his work *The Interpreter of Desires*, banned by the orthodox authorities but embraced by many as a masterpiece of spiritual literature. His fame spreads throughout the Muslim world.

1198 Averroes (Faylasuf Ibn Rushd), famous philosopher and theologian who applies the ideas of Aristotle and Plato to Islamic thought, dies in Cordoba, Spain. He writes many scholarly commentaries and treatises that present Aristotle's thought to the Islamic world and are also influential among Jews and Christians. He champions the use of reason and logical proof in determining religious law (*sharī'a*) and remains one of Islam's greatest thinkers.

The Life of Saint Francis

Francis of Assisi (c. 1181–1226) is the son of a wealthy merchant who receives a good education but is rebellious in his youth, engaging in drinking and merrymaking. He becomes a soldier and after serving in a local war between Assisi and Perugia, is taken prisoner. While held captive, he becomes ill and has a vision calling him to religious life, and thereafter he devotes his life to poverty and charity. After founding the Franciscan orders, he continues to travel and preach until, in the last years of his life, he withdraws from public activity and enters seclusion. He's said to have experienced a vision of the cross that leaves him with physical stigmata or wounds of Christ. He remains one of the most beloved of Christian saints, known for his simple piety expressed in love of animals and the poor.

1204 Constantinople is sacked during the Fourth Crusade, called in 1202 by Pope Innocent III who had hoped to invade the Holy Land through Egypt.

1209 The Albigensian Crusade is called by Pope Innocent III to eradicate the Albigensian heresy. Lasting several decades, the struggle largely represents the resistance by local rulers to papal control. At last, after bloody struggle, the heresy is eliminated and Southern France comes under control of the Church.

1200

1206 Because the heretical Albigensian (or Cathar) sect has gained favor with the people of southern France, St. Dominic resolves to convert the heretics, noting the failure of the Papal Legates to do so by orthodox means. The Albigensians engage in extreme ascetic practices of denying the body and its desires as evil. Since Dominic is known for his asceticism—wearing hair shirts and walking barefoot—he appeals to them on their level and meets with some success, but not enough as the schism persists. He also founds the Roman Catholic Order of Preachers (the Dominican Order) in 1215.

1209 Saint Francis of Assisi receives papal approval from Innocent III to found a new religious order, the Order of Friars Minor. He later founds orders for women (known popularly as the "Poor Claires") and laypeople. Commonly called Franciscans, these monks, nuns, and laypersons live by the principle of the imitation of Christ. After his many missionary journeys, his order grows to include thousands of members.

1212 Though the Children's Crusade is probably a legend, tradition holds that a boy begins preaching in France or Germany, claiming that Jesus has commanded him to lead a Crusade to the Holy Land. Through a show of miracles, he gains a following of thousands of children en route to the Mediterranean, where he claims the sea will part. When this doesn't occur, the children board merchant ships and are shipwrecked or sold into slavery in Africa.

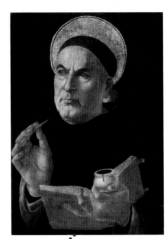

1224–1274 Life of Saint Thomas Aquinas, foremost theologian of the Roman Catholic Church. A Dominican monk and professor of theology, Aquinas is a proponent of Aristotelian logic and the role of reason in ascertaining theological truth. He seeks to reconcile faith and reason in a systematic theology and is the founder of the Thomistic school. Although his views meet with resistance from the Church, he's canonized in 1323 and remains one of the most influential Christian theologians. Among his numerous works is the *Summa Theologiae*.

c. 1220 Nalanda, the great monastic university in Bihar, Northern India, is destroyed during Mongol raids. Built in the 5th century during the Gupta period, Nalanda was a great center of learning which attracted many famous scholars and pilgrims, such as the Chinese monk Hsüan Tsang.

1231 Pope Gregory IX institutes the Papal Inquisition for the arrest and trial of heretics, in response to the growing heresies of the Albigensians (Cathars) and Waldenses, a sect devoted to living in poverty.

1236 Dōgen founds the Sōtō school of Zen Buddhism in Japan. At a young age he became a monk at the famous Mt. Hiei monastery, but became dissatisfied with the teachings, and went to China in search of the pure doctrine, studying meditation under Ch'an masters. On his return to Japan, he spreads the teachings and founds a temple at Eihei. His most famous work is the *Shobogenzo*, which sets forth his understanding of enlightenment. The Sōtō school emphasizes *zazen* meditation as the chief practice.

c. 1270 *Sepher ha Zohar* (*Book of Splendor*) is composed by Moses de León, Jewish mystic of Guadalajara, Spain, the center of Kabbalah mysticism. The text is regarded as the core scripture of Kabbalah and is traditionally said to be based on the earlier version of the *Zohar* by 2nd century Simeon bar Yohai. It presents a mystical view of creation by means of the 10 *sephirot* or divine emanations. The teachings of the Kabbalah gain wide popularity after the expulsion of the Jews from Spain in 1492.

1253 Nichiren, charismatic Buddhist leader and founder of a Pure Land school in Japan, proclaims that the Lotus Sutra contains all the teachings of Buddhism and that chanting its name alone is sufficient to grant salvation. For the next 30 years Nichiren spreads his radical message, declaring all other teachings false. He's exiled twice by the government and attacked by rivals. A controversial figure, his message is militant and apocalyptic. However, his teaching remains influential to this day in modern Pure Land sects that trace their lineage to him.

1273 Death of Jalal al-Din al-Rumi, Persian Sufi mystic and poet. His greatest work is the *Verses of Spiritual Meaning* (*Masnavī-ye Ma'navi*) containing over 25,000 verses. After Rumi's death, his disciples organize into the Mawlawīya order, popularly known as the "whirling dervishes" because of the circular dance that is their spiritual practice. The poetry of Rumi continues to inspire, enjoying a great renaissance among English speakers today.

1329 Meister Eckhart (Johannes Eckhart), German Dominican theologian and mystic, is charged with heresy by Pope John XXII. A professor of theology who is influenced by the rational philosophy of Thomas Aquinas, he writes a number of treatises based on personal experience in which he outlines the stages of union between the soul and God, stating that the soul must ultimately abandon even God in its journey. Though he formally recants his views before his death, they continue to influence thinkers to this day.

1391–1474 Life of Gyalwa Gendün Drupa, first Dalai Lama of Tibet, disciple of Tsong Khapa. Gendün Drupa oversees the construction of Ganden monastery near Lhasa, and founds Tashilhunpo monastery in central Tibet.

1300

1357–1419 Life of Tsong Khapa, Buddhist saint and reformer, founder of the Gelugpa order of Dalai Lamas. At a time when discipline has become lax in Tibet, Tsong Khapa implements comprehensive religious reform that establishes the institutional foundation for Buddhism in Tibet into the 20th century. A famous teacher and scholar, he establishes the monastery of Ganden outside of Lhasa and the Monlam Chenmo, or Great Prayer Festival, which brings thousands of pilgrims from all over Tibet together each year in Lhasa. He also writes numerous volumes of scriptural commentary, one of his greatest being the *Lam Rim Chenmo* (*Great Path Stages*), which synthesizes the different schools and practices of Buddhism into a comprehensive system. Among his disciples are Gyalwa Gendün Drupa, who will become the first Dalai Lama.

1380 English theologian John Wycliffe organizes the first complete translation of the Bible into English. Widely regarded as a forerunner of the Reformation, he criticizes the teachings of the Roman Catholic Church and believes that each person should be able to read the scriptures in his native tongue. The Wycliffe Bible, though condemned in 1382, survives in scattered copies and remains an important scriptural source until the King James Bible is published in 1611.

The Dalai Lamas

The Dalai Lamas are a lineage of reincarnated masters (*tulku*) of the Gelugpa order of Tibetan Buddhism. Each of the 14 Dalai Lamas to date is regarded as a reincarnation of the same divine being, the Buddhist deity of compassion, Avalokitesvara. From the 17th century until the Chinese invasion of Tibet in 1959, the Dalai Lamas were the temporal and spiritual heads of Tibet, ruling from the Potala palace in Lhasa. The word *Dalai* means "ocean" in Mongolian, *Lama* means "spiritual teacher," and *Dalai Lama* ("ocean of wisdom") was first given to the 3rd Dalai Lama, Sonam Gyatso, by Mongolian ruler Altai Khan in the 16th century. Upon the death of a Dalai Lama, his reincarnation is sought by senior monks who consult a variety of oracles. Young boys who are likely candidates are sometimes asked to identify items that belonged to the previous Dalai Lama. The successful candidate is then brought to Lhasa and educated by the finest tutors, a process that typically lasts upward of 20 years.

1440–1518 Life of Kabir, Indian poet and mystic, who merges Hindu and Sufi mysticism in his devotional poems and songs which speak of oneness among men and laying aside doctrine for direct experience of God. He rejects the caste system and refuses to identify himself as Hindu or Muslim. He's a weaver by trade and composes his poems orally in common Hindi. His poems are later collected in the work titled *Bijak* (*Seedling*).

1415 Czech religious reformer Jan Hus is burned at the stake. A university professor and preacher influenced by the radical thought of John Wycliffe, Hus begins to speak out against the corruption of the Roman Catholic clergy. Running afoul of the local archbishop and ordered to stop preaching, Hus is excommunicated when he refuses and is put on trial for heresy. Arrested at the Council of Constance, he defends his views and is executed.

1431 Joan of Arc, saint of the Roman Catholic Church and national heroine of France, dies. A peasant girl who receives divine visions and leads the French army to victory at Orleans during the Hundred Years War, she's burned at the stake as a heretic after being taken prisoner by the English.

1455 The first Vulgate Bible is printed by Johannes Gutenberg, inventor of movable type. At a time when books are reproduced by hand, Gutenberg is able to produce approximately 180 copies on paper and vellum in a 3-year period, a great advance in productivity. Chapter headings are illuminated by hand in red ink. Approximately 60 copies survive to the present day.

1469–1539 Life of Guru Nanak, founder of the Sikh religion. Born a Hindu in India, in his young adulthood Nanak has a religious experience that causes him to leave his life as a storekeeper and travel for 20 years. He eventually purchases land and establishes a community for his followers. Influenced heavily by both Hinduism and Islam, Nanak teaches a monotheistic faith that emphasizes the unity of God and man's moral obligation to live righteously. He rejects asceticism, teaching the values of charity and service. He composes some 400 hymns, which contain the essence of his teachings, compiled in the Adi Granth ("Original Book") the central scripture of the Sikh religion.

1450

1478 Pope Sixtus IV authorizes the Spanish Inquisition at the request of the Spanish Crown as a tool to suppress heretics, Jews, and Muslims. After the first Inquisitors prove unrestrained, the Pope intervenes and appoints the first grand inquisitor, Dominican cleric Tomás de Torquemada, who acquires a reputation for extracting forced confessions by torture. Up to 2,000 heretics are burned at the stake. The Inquisition lasts in modified forms until 1834.

1463 Translation of *Corpus Hermeticum* from Greek into Latin by Renaissance scholar Marsilio Ficino, a member of the court of Cosimo de Medici. The Hermetic texts are mystical writings dating from late antiquity attributed to the god Hermes Trismegistus or "Thrice Great" considered identical with the Egyptian god Thoth. Among texts are *Poimandres* and *Asclepius*. The collection, published in 1471, has a major influence on Renaissance culture, providing a basis for the Hermetic tradition of magic and alchemy.

1486 A manual for witch hunters, the *Malleus Maleficarum* (*Hammer of Witches*) is written by two Dominican theologians, Johann Sprenger and Heinrich Kraemer, who claimed the sanction of Pope Innocent VIII. Used to suppress witchcraft in Germany, their manual details the believed behavior of witches, including consorting with demons, nocturnal flights, and shape-shifting. It also discusses legal procedures for trying witches, including the use of torture to extract confessions. The book is in wide use into the 18th century.

1492 Ferdinand II and Isabella, Catholic monarchs of Spain, issue the Alhambra Decree ordering the expulsion of Jews following victory over the Moors at the Battle of Granada. About 70,000 Jews convert to Christianity, and approximately 130,000 enter exile. The Sephardim, or Spanish Jews, settle largely in North Africa and southeastern Europe. Regarded by Jews as the most tragic exile since the 1st-century diaspora after the fall of Rome, the expulsion marks the beginning of centuries of persecution in Europe.

1498 Death of Girolamo Savonarola, Italian Dominican reformer and martyr. Outspoken against both the Renaissance humanism that he views as licentious and the corruption of the Church in Rome, Savonarola gains great fame as a theologian, preaching the need for religious reform. When Medici power in Florence crumbles, Savonarola becomes the ruler of the city, implementing his policies, including the "bonfire of the vanities," a collecting and burning of "sinful" objects such as cosmetics, artworks, and manuscripts. Among the destroyed objects are works by the painter Botticelli. However, his enemies gain power and, in alliance with the corrupt Pope Alexander VI, have Savonarola silenced, then tried and executed.

Modern Religion: Reformation and Enlightenment, 1500–1900

In this period, our attention is drawn largely to Europe, as the revolutionary developments of the Reformation ushered in the modern era, in many ways shaping the contours of the contemporary religious landscape.

In the larger sense, this period following the Middle Ages may be considered the beginning of modernity. It is commonly thought to have begun with the European discovery of movable type and the printing press, technology that greatly accelerated the rate of cultural dissemination and change. The modern era is characterized by the increasing role of science and technology, mass literacy, urbanization, industrialization, the rise of capitalism, of the nation-state, and of representative democracy. In an increasingly bureaucratic and secular world, rational attitudes reign supreme, inspiring the counterreaction of the Romantic movement, which champions the intuitive and emotional sensibilities. This tension between rational and romantic outlooks is echoed throughout much of the modern period.

The defining event of this period was the Protestant Reformation, effectively set in motion by Martin Luther at the beginning of the sixteenth century, and soon taken up by such figures as Calvin and Zwingli, and echoed in the creation of the Anglican church by English King Henry VIII. A movement rather than a single, organized body, the Reformation reflected widespread social and economic changes in Europe and challenged the authority of Pope and Church, stressing the role of individual faith in salvation and the right of each individual to interpret scripture, which became possible with the technology of printing and the translation of the Bible into German and shortly after, into English. Protestantism continues to be a dynamic force to the present day, giving rise to many sects that differ in their interpretation of the Christian message.

In America, Protestant sects such as the Puritans and Quakers flourished, and new forms of Christianity such as Mormonism and Christian Science arose in the fresh soil of the emerging nation. These developments were a major driving force in American culture, and such social movements as the Great Awakening of the early eighteenth century, and the Second Great Awakening at the end of that century under the leadership of such charismatic figures as Jonathan Edwards and Charles Finney (respectively) spearheaded a popular revival of religion in America. Such figures as Finney and John Nelson Darby, an English evangelist, popularized the literal interpretation of scripture during this period, establishing a fundamentalist movement that had great influence on American Protestantism.

In India, China, and Japan, Western colonial influence resulted in cultural tension as Christian missionaries and local European governments forced traditional religions to adapt and reformulate their identities. In India, the Moghul dynasty reached great heights of cultural achievement with such architectural masterpieces as the Taj Mahal and explored the sensitive relationship between Hindu and Muslim faiths. In China, Neo-Confucianism continued to develop, and popular uprisings such as the Taoist Taiping Rebellion occurred. In Japan, this era saw the great feudal shoguns and their Zen samurai, and in the nineteenth century the Meiji Restoration, which implemented State Shinto and the Emperor cult, contributes to Japan's ambivalent relationship with Western colonial powers and lays the ground-work for the later events of World War II.

In Central and South America, colonialism also shaped religious history as European powers (in particular, the Spanish) conquered the great empires of the Aztecs and Incas, aggressively assimilating the native traditions and imposing Catholicism. The native traditions were often driven underground and mixed with Christian elements.

This era was a defining one for the Jewish faith, exhibiting the tension between rationalism and mysticism typical of modernity. The great champions of rationalism, such as the philosophers Baruch Spinoza and Moses Mendelssohn, interpreted the Torah according to reason and made an appeal for the Jewish people to be included in mainstream society in accord with emerging ideals of democracy. On the other hand, the mystical pole was represented by the great popularity of Kabbalah mysticism and by such teachers as Isaac Luria and Bal Shem Tov, founder of the Hasidic movement. Mass

messianic movements of such figures as Shabbati Sevi and Jacob Frank channeled the popular sentiments of the people in an age of uncertainty.

Catholicism also saw defining developments during this period. The Counter-Reformation, a response to the challenge of the Reformation, largely succeeded in addressing the doctrinal and institutional lapses that had caused widespread disillusionment with the Church and restored popular faith. Religious leaders such as Francis Xavier, a great missionary, and St. John of the Cross, a Spanish mystic, helped rejuvenate the spiritual vitality of the Catholic tradition and assure its foothold in the colonies and the New World.

Another distinctive facet of the modern era was the first widespread assimilation of Eastern religions in the West. A by-product of colonial presence in the Orient was increasing knowledge of these traditions in Europe and America. The first Indian teachers of yoga came to America as well as the first teachers of Zen Buddhism. Popular movements that drew heavily on Eastern traditions enjoyed immense popularity, most notably the Theosophical movement of Madame Blavatsky.

All of these strands of modernity—the pull of secularization, of fundamentalism, and the tension between the rational and mystical —continue to intensify throughout the period. We'll see in the next section how they are still winding through the religious landscape to this very day.

1506 Wang Yang Ming, Neo-Confucian philosopher and statesman, has a pivotal revelation while on government assignment in a remote area of China—that the principles of things are to be found within one's own mind, rather than in external objects—an idealist position opposed to the prevailing rationalism of the time. A renowned teacher with many disciples of his unique philosophy, he dies while returning from suppressing a rebellion. His main work is the *Instructions for Practical Living* (*Ch'uan-hsi lu*). His philosophy has influenced many generations of Chinese philosophers

1517 Tradition holds that on October 31 Martin Luther posts his *Ninety-five Theses* on the door of the castle church at Wittenberg, marking the start of the Protestant Reformation. The *Theses* condemn the excesses of the Catholic Church and spread quickly through Germany, rousing widespread demand for religious reform and greater freedom from Rome.

Martin Luther

Already in his 30s and leading a pious life as an Augustinian monk and professor of theology, Luther has a spiritual breakthrough following his observation of the papal sale of religious indulgences (certificates of merit issued by the Pope, which could in part nullify sins, sold for money to pious Christians), the funds from which are used for excessive pomp in Rome. His *Ninety-five Theses*, which is a call to debate the theological grounds for this practice, spreads quickly through Germany facilitated by the printing press, which is hard-pressed to keep up with demand. Luther's beliefs continue to develop, reaching their apex around 1518 in his conviction that salvation comes through the grace of God, not by human effort; faith alone brings justification. Reflecting the spirit of the times, popular support for Luther continues to increase. His career can be regard-ed as the opening salvo of the Reformation, a call for reform of the Church, heralded by widespread changes in society in the later Middle Ages.

1500

1508 Michelangelo is commissioned by Pope Julius II to paint the Sistine Chapel ceiling in the Vatican, an effort that takes 4 years and requires the invention of special scaffolds and plaster by the master. When finished, the work depicts over 300 biblical figures and scenes. The nudity of figures offends some pious clergy and a campaign is launched to remove the frescoes; Michelangelo responds by portraying one of his critics, Biagio da Cesena, in the scenes as Minos, judge of the underworld. Nude figures are later covered by artist Daniele da Volterra.

1517 The Ottoman ruler Selim I captures Jerusalem from the Egyptian Mamluk Sultinate. Under the rule of his son, Suleiman the Magnificent (reigned 1520–1566), a wall is rebuilt around the Old City to restore a portion of its former glory.

1521 In response to Luther's *Ninety-five Theses*, Pope Leo X issues a bull of condemnation formally excommunicating Luther. He's called before the Imperial Diet of Worms and given the chance to recant but refuses to go against his conscience. While the Diet is deliberating, Luther disappears, secretly apprehended by his protector, the elector Frederick, and is kept in seclusion in Wartburg Castle.

1521 Aztec capital Tenochtitlan is destroyed by Spanish conquistadors led by Hernan Cortes. It's thought to have been one of the largest and most splendid cities in the world when, according to accounts of conquistadors, the Aztec ruler Moctezuma II mistakes Cortes for the god Quetzalcoatl. He receives Cortes with great ceremony, only to have him conquer Tenochtitlan after a prolonged siege during which much of the city is destroyed. Mexico City is later built on the site of the ruins.

1522 Luther translates the New Testament into German during his seclusion at Wartburg Castle. In 1534, he completes translation of the entire Bible.

The Protestant Reformation

The work of Martin Luther is soon echoed by Zwingli, Calvin, and other religious reformers who bring about a revisioning of Christianity and a split with the Roman Catholic Church that remains definitive to this day. A constellation of factors are behind this, including a growing concentration of populations in towns and cities; the consequent rise of a cash economy as well as a middle class that's independent from feudal lords; the tradition of humanism brought on by the Renaissance with its rediscovery of Classical learning and expansion of the known world through the explorations of Marco Polo, Columbus, and others; and a growing discontent of princely rulers of Northern Europe about being under the yoke of Rome. These cultural changes are reflected in the theology of Luther and others, which is critical of the Pope's authority and the dogma and sacraments of the Church and emphasizes the role of individual faith and the individual's right to read and interpret scripture for himself. Protestantism is a movement that encompasses many factions and the following centuries will see the formation and splintering of many denominations under the Protestant umbrella.

1522 Catholic pastor Huldrych Zwingli initiates the Swiss Reformation with a series of influential sermons. The following year his *Sixty-seven Artikel* is published criticizing the Church, and his reforms are officially adopted by local civic and religious authorities. A contemporary of Luther, he reaches many parallel conclusions, and his reforms include abolishing the celibacy of priests, removing images and music from churches, revision

of the sacraments of mass and baptism, and return to the Bible as scriptural source. However, Zwingli disputes with the Anabaptists as well as Martin Luther on theological points, and consequently, his doctrines are never endorsed by the Lutherans.

1525

1525 First Anabaptist ("rebaptizer") adult baptisms are held outside Zurich, led by Konrad Grebel and others. The Anabaptists are a Reformation sect that denies the legitimacy of infant baptism as a sacrament of the Church and hold that

one can only truly be baptized through an act of free will. Holding apocalyptic beliefs, they seek to restore the purity of the church and overturn civic order. Considered heretical by the Catholic Church, and persecuted by the authorities who view their revolutionary doctrines as a threat, many are imprisoned or put to death. The original movement Splits into numerous sects, some pacifist, some militant. Present-day Amish, Hutterites, and Mennonites are descended from Anabaptist groups.

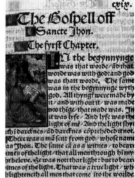

1525 The New Testament is translated into English by William Tyndale. A scholar and university instructor educated at Oxford and Cambridge, Tyndale is influenced by Protestant ideas and resolves to translate the Bible so it can be read by the common man. Because his work is considered heretical by the Church of England, he leaves for Germany in 1524 to pursue it. There he's influenced by the work of Martin Luther and completes the first portion of the Bible to be printed in English, the New Testament. He goes on to work on the Old Testament, completing the Pentateuch and several other biblical books. He's arrested in 1535 in Belgium by order of Henry VIII, tried, and burned at the stake for heresy. The King James Bible is based largely on his translations.

1531 Legend records that Juan Diego Cuauhtlatoatzin sees an apparition of the Virgin of Guadalupe on Tepeyac hill near Mexico City December 9–12. He's on his way to Catholic church when he has a vision of birds singing and a luminous lady calling to him. She identifies herself as the Virgin Mary and asks him to tell Bishop Juan de Zumarraga her wishes

for a temple on that spot where she'll grant healing to the people of Mexico. She tells him to gather roses in his cloak as a sign for the bishop, and when the cloak is unfolded, the image of Our Lady of Guadalupe, Mexico's most popular religious image, is emblazoned on it. Patron saint of America, she's regarded by Catholics as a manifestation of the Virgin Mary and may also be a form of the native goddess Tonantzin.

1533 Atahualpa, the last Inca emperor, is killed by command of Spanish conquistador Francisco Pizarro. On his way to the Inca capital at Cusco with his army, Atahualpa meets Pizarro's company, numbering just 168 men, who demand their conversion to Christianity. Atahualpa refuses, throwing the Bible on the ground, causing the Spanish to retaliate. During the Battle of Cajamarca on November 16, 1532, thousands of Inca soldiers are killed within a few hours and Atahualpa is imprisoned in the Temple of the Sun. The ruler offers to pay a room full of gold and twice as much silver for his release, but Pizarro eventually decides to execute him. Just before his death, Atahualpa converts to Christianity to avoid being burned, which according to Inca belief would mean destruction of the soul.

1534 King Henry VIII, angered by Pope Clement VII's refusal to grant him a divorce from Catharine of Aragon, rejects Papal authority "and establishes the Church of England with the King as supreme head. Shortly afterward, "the first

liturgy in English is composed, the *Book of Common Prayer*.

1534 Isaac Luria, founder of the Lurianic school of Kabbalah, is born in Jerusalem. Based on the *Sefer-ha-Zohar*, the Lurianic account of creation holds that God (*Ein Soph*) "withdraws" into himself to make room for creation (*tzimtzum*). A divine beam of light pervades the space and is encapsulated in "vessels" of form, which crack under the strain, and disharmony enters the world. Mankind's role is to participate in the redemption (*tikkun*) of the world, returning the divine sparks to the Creator and restoring Adam Qadmon, the primordial man. The Kabbalist helps do this through the use of prayers, rituals, and formulas of sacred words. Lurianic Kabbalah will become the most influential thread in Jewish mysticism, influencing, for one, the Hasidic movement of the 18th century.

Inca Culture, 1438–1533

The Inca Empire had a rich spiritual tradition that centered around worship of the sun. Inti, the sun god, ancestor of the Inca, and bringer of warmth was the foremost deity. Viracocha was the creator-god of earth, man, and animals. Many other gods and goddesses of earth, sky, and the natural world populated the Inca pantheon. Temples were constructed throughout the empire to honor these gods, the most famous being the Sun Temple at Cusco. An elaborate hierarchy of priests, presided over by a high priest, relative of the king, served the temples along with a group of Chosen Women picked at childhood for their beauty, who were occasionally sacrificed to the gods. Sacrifices of humans and animals were performed to honor the movements of the sun and key dates in the sacred 30-day calendar. A variety of methods were used to consult with gods on all important decisions, including speaking to the deities through sacred images, reading patterns on the organs of sacrificed animals or in the arrangement of leaves, and imbibing the hallucinogenic potion ayahuasca.

1535 After the death of members of his congregation in a failed Anabaptist revolt, Dutch Catholic priest Menno Simons begins to preach against the Catholic Church, articulating his beliefs in nonviolence, scriptural authority, baptism on confession of faith, and a symbolic understanding of the Eucharist. Around 1537 he receives believer's baptism, and formally becomes an Anabaptist leader. His followers, called Mennonites, spread across Northern Europe and, in the 17th century, to North America.

1537 The first printed version of the complete Bible in English, known as the Matthew Bible, is published under the pseudonym Thomas Matthew. It incorporates translations by three authors: William Tyndale (whose New Testament was published previously), Myles Coverdale, and John Rogers. Tyndale and Rogers are burned at the stake for their heresy; Coverdale goes on to compile the Great Bible in 1539 under Sir Thomas Cromwell, the first English translation of the Bible officially authorized by the Church of England.

1542 Pope Paul III founds the Congregation of the Holy Office, the authoritative court in matters of heresy, marking the beginning of the Roman Inquisition. Among the heretics tried are occultist Giordano Bruno and astronomer Galileo Galilei, who is condemned in 1633 for his defense of Copernicus' theory that the Earth revolves around the Sun. These efforts are part of the Counter-Reformation, the Roman Catholic Church's internal reform and response to the threat of the Protestant Reformation.

1536 John Calvin—founder of Calvinism and the second most important figure of the Protestant Reformation, after Martin Luther—publishes the first edition of his *Institutes of the Christian Religion*. Born in France and educated in theology and the traditions of Renaissance humanism, he later moves to Basel, Switzerland where he's influenced by Protestant ideas and writes the *Institutes*. He becomes a leading figure in the Reformation in Switzerland, waging a political and theological battle against opposing religious factions. In accord with Reformation ideas, his reforms include the endorsement of marriage for clergy and the establishment of a new ecclesiastical hierarchy. By 1555, Calvinist doctrine gains supremacy in Switzerland.

1541 Spaniard Saint Francis Xavier, great Roman Catholic missionary, leaves on his journey to India, Malaysia, and Japan. He's one of the first 7 members of the Society of Jesus, or Jesuits under Saint Ignatius of Loyola, to take vows of poverty, celibacy, and missionary service. First spending several years among Indian villagers, he baptizes thousands before traveling to Malaysia where he establishes a number of missions. Returning to India in 1548, he trains new missionary priests at the College of St. Paul in Goa. In 1549, Xavier travels to Japan where he gains about 2,000 converts. Tens of thousands of people are converted through his work, making him responsible for more conversions than anyone besides the Apostle Paul, according to the Catholic Church. He's made a saint in 1622 by Pope Gregory XV.

1542–1591   Life of St. John of the Cross, Spanish mystic and poet. A Carmelite priest, he assists St. Theresa of Avila in reforming the Carmelite order, forming the Discalced, or Barefoot, Carmelite Order. Meeting with opposition, he's imprisoned 1577–1578, during which time he writes his poetic masterpiece, the *Spiritual Canticle*, describing in allegorical fashion the soul's yearning for God in the manner of a bride yearning for her bridegroom. After escaping from prison, he attains high office in the Order and continues to write and found monasteries. His *Dark Night of the Soul* describes the stages of the soul's ascent in its union with God. These poems are considered to be among the finest Spanish mystical literature.

1554   The Mayan *Popul Vuh* (*Council Book*) is written in Spanish script in the Guatemalan language of Quiché. It records ancient oral Mayan creation myths, stories of the gods, and the history of the Quiché kingdom. Written in secret after the native hieroglyphic script is banned by the Spanish, it's discovered in 1702 by a local priest, Francisco Ximenez, who translates it into Spanish.

1560–1605
Akbar the Great, emperor of the Islamic Mughul dynasty in India, extends Mughul power over much of Northern India. Akbar is known for his religious tolerance, and since the Mughul dynasty contains both Muslims and Hindus, he appoints Hindus to high office and implements nondiscriminatory policies. He builds a House of Worship where he sponsors debates between Muslims, Hindus, and Christians and is conversant with literature of Jains, Zoroastrians, and others. His tolerance, however, provokes resentment among Muslims in the empire, and Hindu-Muslim relations deteriorate in coming generations.

1545–1563   The Council of Trent is convened by Pope Paul III to address the issues of the Counter-Reformation. The Council responds to the Protestant doctrines of Luther and Zwingli by implementing reforms in doctrine addressing the role of faith and the sacraments and in the training and appointment of clergy, limiting the excesses of the previous era.

1560   Scottish Parliament votes to establish Protestantism as national religion under leadership of John Knox, chief reformer of the Church of Scotland.

73

1578 Mongol chief Altan Khan bestows the honorary title of Dalai Lama ("ocean of wisdom") onto Sönam Gyatso, head of the Gelugpa order of Tibetan Buddhism. (The title is posthumously applied to his two predecessors, thus making him the 3rd Dalai Lama). Alliance with the Mongols gives the Dalai Lama and the Gelugpa order significant power, and from the 17th century, the Dalai Lama becomes civil and spiritual leader of Tibet.

1600 Jakob Böhme, German mystic and cobbler by trade, has a vision. Hearing a sermon by charismatic Lutheran preacher Martin Möller in his town

of Görlitz, Böhme has a spiritual illumination that he believes gives profound insight into the nature of the cosmos and good and evil. After contemplating privately for a decade, he relates his insights in a manuscript, the *Aurora*. The chief pastor of Görlitz, Gregorious Richter, learns of the contents and prohibits Böhme from writing upon threat of exile. A number of years later, however, Böhme writes the *Way to Christ* (1623) and spends the last year of his life in exile. Among the ideas found in his works is the heretical notion that the Fall represents a necessary stage in the evolution of the world.

1600

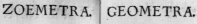

1600 Giordano Bruno, Italian philosopher, astronomer, occultist, and Dominican priest, is burned at the stake for heresy. Regarded as one of the great hermetic philosophers of the Renaissance, Bruno is famous for his prodigious memory. Traveling to Switzerland, France, England, Germany, and Italy to avoid excommunication and trouble with the authorities, he writes prolifically and publishes over 20 books. He's arrested in Italy in 1592, charged with heresy, imprisoned for 6 years, and 8 years later executed for his Neoplatonic pantheistic theological beliefs.

1609 General Baptist church founded by Anglican priest John Smyth when he

leaves the Church of England, adopting the belief in adult baptism and religious liberty. He later has a falling out with colleague Thomas Helwys, an influential leader of the Baptists. Smyth's ideas influence the Pilgrim fathers who come to North America in search of religious freedom in 1620.

1604 Canonical version of the Adi Granth, Sikh holy scripture, is compiled by Guru Arjan Dev, the 5th Sikh Guru. He also builds the Golden Temple at Amritsar, Northern India, spiritual center of the Sikh religion, completed in 1601.

1620 Pilgrims land at Cape Cod and establish the Plymouth Colony. A group of religious separatists from the Church of England led by Rev. William Brewster and John Carver, the original group of 102 sailed for America on the *Mayflower* seeking a place to practice their religion in peace.

1611 King James Version of the Bible is published in English under "King James I" or "England for the Church of England." Until this time, translating the Bible into English has been a capital offense. The effort, which took almost 50 scholars 7 years to complete, is a benchmark of English literary style and remains the standard English Bible until the 20th century.

1631 Construction begins on the Taj Mahal (completed in 1654). It's commissioned by Muslim Emperor Shah Jahan of the Mughul dynasty, who builds it as a mausoleum for his wife, Mumtaz. Under his reign, Mughul achievements in architecture reach their highest point.

1642 Mongol leader Gushri Khan gains control of Tibet and appoints Ngawang Losang Gyatso 5th Dalai Lama. Known commonly as the "Great Fifth," he establishes the political supremacy of the Gelugpa order and builds the Potala palace in Lhasa, traditional residence of the Dalai Lama.

1649 George Fox founds the Society of Friends, or Quakers. An unschooled cobbler's apprentice and shepherd, he leaves home as a young man in search of religious truth. His many disillusioning encounters with clergy and personal revelations, or "openings," convince him that the truth of Christian teachings lies in the "inward light" rather than Church creeds and ceremonies. He gathers a loyal following but also attracts the hostility of authorities due to his rejection of established religious creeds and civil obligations such as serving in the military. He's arrested and imprisoned many times. He makes missionary journeys to Ireland, the Caribbean, and the North American colonies, where the Quaker movement flourishes.

1650

1648 Perhaps as many as 200,000 Jews are killed in the Chmielnicki Cossack uprising, a civil war in the Polish-Lithuanian commonwealth. Eastern Slavic leader Bohdan Chmielnicki heads this anti-Semitic campaign to restore ethnic autonomy from perceived Polish and Jewish control.

1656 Dutch rationalist philosopher Baruch Spinoza is excommunicated from the Jewish community for his pantheistic claims that God equals nature and the Bible is allegorical. His greatest work, the *Ethics*, relies on reason to determine ethical truth and states that good and bad are relative. He has great influence on Enlightenment thinkers and is regarded as one of the pioneers of biblical criticism.

1658–1707 Reign of emperor Aurangzeb, last great Mughul emperor, who attempts to convert all India to Islam. Although his predecessors, notably Akbar, had promoted cultural and religious tolerance, Aurangzeb, a pious Sunni Muslim, implements harsh non-Hindu policies and destroys hundreds of Hindu temples, building mosques on the foundations. His brutal religious repression and military campaigns backfire, and his vassals, many of them Hindu, begin to rebel, marking the start of the decline of the Moghul dynasty. Aurangzeb's policies leave a legacy of religious sectarianism in India that echoes to the present day.

1666 Imprisonment in Constantinople of Shabbetai Zevi, messianic figure and leader of mass movement among European Jews. As a youth in Turkey, Shabbetai studies Kabbalah and has frequent ecstatic episodes. Proclaiming himself Messiah, many followers are drawn to his personal magnetism. Banished, he wanders through the Mediterranean region, attaining support of rabbis who vouch that he's the Messiah, then marches triumphantly to Jerusalem, proclaiming 1666 as the year of the apocalypse and restoration of Israel. Arrested by authorities at Constantinople, he's brought before the sultan, and under pain of torture, converts to Islam, thus dashing the messianic hopes of most of his Jewish followers.

1662 First poems of Zen poet Bashō, known for developing the haiku form of poetry into a spiritual art form. Born into the samurai class, when his master dies, Bashō moves to Kyoto where he lives in a simple meditation hut and goes on frequent journeys by foot, composing poems and diaries of his travels.

1686-1769 Life of Japanese Zen monk, writer, and artist Hakuin, credited with reviving the Rinzai school of Zen Buddhism. A monk by about age 15, he soon becomes disillusioned with existing Buddhist teachings and takes up the wandering life, having a number of enlightenment experiences. At age 31 he returns to his home temple, becomes abbot, and devotes his life to simple living, teaching, and serving his many students. He promotes the use of *koans*, enigmatic statements for meditation, originating the famous "What is the sound of one hand clapping?" He teaches that direct experience of satori, or enlightenment, is possible for all.

1692 Witch trials occur in Puritan colony of Salem, Massachusetts. After 8 young women display symptoms of fits, babbling, and wild behavior, 19 people are executed, mostly by hanging, and many more imprisoned. Trials are headed by William Stoughton, who allows hearsay as evidence and permits the accused no defense. All who are tried are convicted and sentenced to death. Populations of local jails swell, and the town's

economy stalls. Trials end in 1693 when royal governor of Massachusetts, Sir William Phips, upset that his wife has been accused, appeals to Boston religious leader Increase Mather. It's been speculated that accused women may have been poisoned by ergot, a grain fungus, which would explain their unusual behavior.

1693 Jacob Amman, Swiss Mennonite elder, founds Amish after breaking with Mennonite leaders over the matter of discipline in the congregation. Many Amish migrate to America in the 18th through 20th centuries, and the movement dies out in Europe. The principal Amish community today is in eastern Pennsylvania.

1700

1720 Great Awakening begins. Popular religious revival, counterpart of the Protestant Pietist movements of Europe, lasts until the 1740s. The movement of Protestant sects, including Congregationalists, Presbyterians, Baptists, and Anglicans, emphasizes direct religious experience and preaches the renewal of the message of Jesus. Often drawing hostility from the religious establishment, charismatic preachers travel throughout the colonies, rousing great emotional fervor. Among

the most famous is Jonathan Edwards, Congregationalist pastor of Northampton, Massachusetts. Several educational institutions are influential in the movement, including Princeton and Rutgers universities.

1733 In Philadelphia, Jesuits establish St. Joseph's Church, the only Roman Catholic church built in the colonies before the Revolutionary War.

1736 Muhammad Ibn Abd al-Wahhab, Arab theologian, founds Wahhabi fundamentalist movement of Sunni Islam. Abd al-Wahhab preaches against what he sees as the excesses of Sufi practice and stresses the return to unity and fundamental principles of Islam. He outlaws such practices as the veneration of saints, decoration of mosques, and innovations in religious doctrine. Expelled from his home in Najd, Arabia, Abd al-Wahhab finds patronage under Saudi chieftain Muhammad bin Saud, who makes Wahhabism the official religion. It's the dominant form of Islam in Saudi Arabia and Qatar today.

1745 Swedish scientist, philosopher, and mystic Emanuel Swedenborg receives the divine call to devote himself to spiritual matters. Based on his conversations with angels and spirits, he believes that God is the divine presence within all creation and that man has fallen away from divine perfection through his egotism. Jesus is the redeeming force that can restore man's divine nature; love is the essence of Christian teachings and the path to God. After his death in 1772, his followers form The Church of the New Jerusalem based on his teachings. Swedenborg has influenced many Western thinkers such as Yeats, Goethe, Kant, and Jung; his best known work is *On Heaven and Its Wonders and on Hell*.

1738 English clergyman John Wesley founds Methodist movement. In London, Wesley has a spiritual illumination while reading the letters of St. Paul, cementing his conviction about salvation through faith. He goes on to preach and found religious societies that emphasize personal moral accountability and social action on issues such as prison reform and abolitionism. The Methodists are the first widely popular evangelical movement in England.

c. 1750 Hasidic movement of Judaism is founded by Polish mystic and healer Israel ben Eliezer, a.k.a. Ba'al Shem Tov ("master of the good name"). An orphan, he eventually becomes an innkeeper and butcher while pursuing mystical contemplation on the Kabbalah. His renown as a folk healer grows, and he's known for his humble dress and demeanor in contrast to the rabbis of the day. His teaching emphasizes the role of joy and of service in the practice of Kabbalah, thus differing from the rationalism of rabbinic Torah study and the asceticism of the previous Kabbalah of Isaac Luria. His teachings become the basis of a popular movement that spreads through Eastern Europe, revitalizing Judaism. Hasidism is practiced today in America and Israel.

1751 Messianic movement of Jacob Frank is founded. In the aftermath of the failed Shabbetai Zevi movement and the Cossack uprisings of 1648, many Eastern European Jews are disillusioned and looking for hope. Frank, a Polish mystic, claims to be the Messiah and the reincarnation of Shabbetai Sevi. He forms an antirabbinical movement that teaches that pious people are not subject to the law of Torah and instead should follow the higher law of the Kabbalah. In 1756 the group is banned by Jewish authorities but protected by the Roman Catholic Church. Frank and his supporters are baptized as Christian but continue their lawless ways, and in 1760 Frank is imprisoned by the Inquisition. Freed in 1773, he proclaims himself baron and is treated as such by his followers. Upon his death, the sect dissolves.

1759 Touro Synagogue is built in Newport, Rhode Island. The oldest synagogue in North America, it's built for the Jeshuat Israel congregation established in 1658, comprised of immigrants from Spain, Portugal, and the American colony of New Amsterdam (present-day New York City). It's mentioned in a letter by George Washington proclaiming religious tolerance and is used as a stop on the Underground Railroad in the 19th century.

1755 German Jewish philosopher Moses Mendelssohn publishes first philosophical works, *Philosophical Conversations* and *Letters on the Emotions*. He's the leader of the Jewish enlightenment (*Haskalah*), which promote the enlightenment values of rationalism. He advocates religious tolerance and does much to free German Jews from the cultural prejudices against them. He reconciles the teachings of Judaism with the application of reason, stating that while knowledge of God is innate and self-evident, worldly knowledge requires the proof of reason.

1774 English Shaker leader Ann Lee and a small group of followers arrive in America and settle near Albany, New York. Known as "Mother Ann," she's regarded as an incarnation of the female aspect of God. The Shakers, or United Society of Believers in Christ's Second Appearing, an offshoot of the Quakers, are a millenarian sect that practices celibacy, engages in an ecstatic form of worship involving trembling, dancing, and speaking in tongues (thus the name "Shaker"), lives communally, and strives for perfection through work. They develop a distinctive aesthetic style (known widely in their music and furniture) that reflects their belief in the beauty of austere simplicity. At its height in the mid-19th century, there are some 6,000 members.

1789–1799
The French Revolution limits the power of the Roman Catholic Church, placing clergy under state control and establishing the Enlightenment ideals of democracy and liberty.

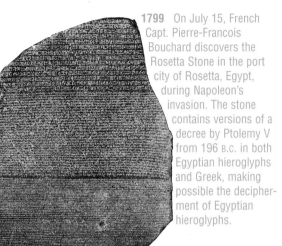

1799   On July 15, French Capt. Pierre-Francois Bouchard discovers the Rosetta Stone in the port city of Rosetta, Egypt, during Napoleon's invasion. The stone contains versions of a decree by Ptolemy V from 196 B.C. in both Egyptian hieroglyphs and Greek, making possible the decipherment of Egyptian hieroglyphs.

1790   Second Great Awakening begins, second popular religious revival in America after the Great Awakening of the 1720s. Movement takes different forms in different regions. In New England, a spirit of social activism leads to founding of religious educational institutions and missions. In Appalachian regions, Methodists and Baptists gain great followings with the camp meeting revival, a several-day gathering of hundreds or thousands of seekers with singing, dancing and preaching that provides a welcome social gathering for frontier folk. Most famous camp revival takes place in Cane Ridge, Kentucky, in 1801, which up to 25,000 people attend.

1799   German theologian Friedrich Schleiermacher publishes *On Religion: Speeches to its Cultured Despisers*, which defends a Romantic approach to religion, harmonizing it with human culture and holding that it's found in the immediate feeling of God. His philosophy of knowledge, influenced by Kant, has a great impact on the field of biblical interpretation. Schleiermacher is an important figure in the development of modern Protestant theology.

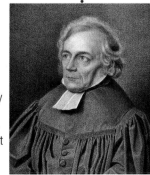

1800–1882 Life of John Nelson Darby, Anglo-Irish fundamentalist preacher, who has a spiritual revelation after falling from a horse that causes him to split from the Church of Ireland. He originates the theory of "dispensationalism," which holds that the Bible tells of seven historical periods, or "dispensations," each followed by destruction. He thus heralds the imminent coming of the apocalypse in the present, 6th era. Also develops the notion of "secret rapture," the belief that Christ will instantly remove true believers from the world during the end times.

1825 British and American Unitarian groups form national associations. Unitarianism flourishes in both England and America, growing out of Calvinist beliefs in the centrality of reason and morals in religion. Unitarianism originally focuses on the unity of God rejecting the notion of the Trinity and the divine identity of Jesus, viewing him rather as a prophet and moral teacher. American Unitarianism grew out of 18th-century Congregationalism and is influenced by the Transcendental movement that focuses on personal experience of the divine. In 1961, American Unitarians merge with the Universalist church. There's no binding creed among Unitarians, and each congregation differs in its practices. Some Unitarians do not consider themselves Christians.

1821 Religious conversion of Charles Finney, central figure in the Second Great Awakening and president of Oberlin College. A lawyer in his early career, he becomes a Presbyterian preacher and uses his oratorical skills to whip crowds into frenzies at religious revivals. He establishes a ministry in New York City and in 1834, breaking with the Presbyterian Church, founds the Broadway Tabernacle.

1828 Hindu religious reformer, Ram Mohun Roy, founds Brahmo Samaj ("Society of Brahman"). Born a Brahmin, Roy develops a philosophy that denounces the divisions present in Indian religion and society under the British raj. He stresses unity of God and the role of reason in attaining religious truth, combining Islamic and Christian elements in his interpretation of Vedanta Hinduism. He travels to England in 1829 as representative of the king of Delhi and is well received. He does much to restore the Hindu tradition in the context of European colonialism.

Mormonism

The Mormon religion originates from the teachings of prophet Joseph Smith, and though Mormonism contains a number of denominations, the majority are members of the Church of Jesus Christ of Latter-Day Saints. Mormon beliefs differ from orthodox Christianity, holding that the persons of the Trinity are separate beings, that human souls have preexisted, and that, after death, spirit and body will reunite eternally and perfectly. Mormons practice baptism, justification by faith, and believe in the individual gift of prophecy as well as the millennial return of Christ to earth. There's no separate priesthood, rather, males at age 12 become novices of the priesthood, ascending through grades, ultimately becoming high priests. Young men are often called to undertake 18 months of missionary work as part of their obligations. Mormons believe in salvation for the dead through baptism, and there has been a traditional interest in genealogy as a way to save deceased ancestors. The Church is centered in Salt Lake City, Utah, and presently has over 9 million members nationwide.

Mormon Polygamy

From the time of Mormon founder Joseph Smith, polygamy has been practiced among the faithful, and is known as "plural marriage." The practice provokes ridicule and persecution by larger society and leads to the federal government enacting anti-polygamy laws in 1862. Polygamy was among the reasons that the Territory of Utah was denied statehood until 1896. The Mormon church officially outlawed polygamy in 1890, but the practice has been followed ever since by religious groups known as "Mormon fundamentalists" that split from the mainstream church and are not regarded as valid by the Church of Jesus Christ of Latter-Day Saints. The practice of polygamy is difficult to prosecute since practitioners are not formally married. Polygamy has been practiced traditionally in religions such as Islam and Hinduism.

1830 The Book of Mormon is published by prophet Joseph Smith and the Mormon church is established at Fayette, New York. Smith, an uneducated farmer, grows up in a region heavily influenced by the Great Awakening revival. While praying in the woods, he has a vision of God and Jesus, and a few years later, the Angel Moroni appears to him, telling him of ancient buried golden plates inscribed with the records of a lost tribe of Israel that came to America in ancient days. The Angel, he claims, shows him the tablets and he translates them into the Book of Mormon, the basis for Mormon beliefs.

1843 Danish Christian philosopher Søren Kierkegaard publishes his work *Either/Or: A Fragment of Life*. He's regarded as the founder of existentialism, which emphasizes the role of free will and personal responsibility in life choices. He examines the psychological nature of freedom and the limits of rationality in understanding existence. He also originates the idea of the "leap of faith," which holds that faith is not primarily rational, but emotional and coexists with doubt. In his later work he's critical of the secularization of the Danish church and calls for a return to stricter Christianity. Kierkegaard's work becomes widely known after World War I.

1844 Brigham Young, senior member of the Mormon church, is chosen to lead the Mormons after founder Joseph Smith and his brother Hyrum are lynched in Carthage, Illinois, by a mob angered over Smith's advocacy of polygamy. Leading the Mormons westward, he settles on the site of Salt Lake City, Utah. Young becomes the governor of the Territory of Utah but is removed from office by federal forces in 1857. He remains head of the Mormon church until his death in 1877. A notorious polygamist, Young has more than 20 wives and scores of children.

1850

1850 Hung Hsiu-ch'üan, a Christian convert who believes he's the Messiah and younger brother of Jesus, leads the Taiping Rebellion against the Chinese Ch'ing dynasty. Arising during a time of great popular unrest, the movement, named the God Worshippers' Society, rises against the imperial army and an estimated 20 million people are killed. Hung then proclaims himself emperor of a new empire, the Heavenly Kingdom of Great Peace, establishing a capital at Nanking. The movement is crushed in 1864, but the Ch'ing dynasty never recovers its former power.

1854 Immaculate conception is declared Catholic dogma by Pope Pius IX. It holds that Mary, mother of Jesus Christ, is freed by God from original sin from the time of her conception. The doctrine has precursors in earlier Christian doctrines but is not declared dogma until this time.

1863 Bahá'u'lláh, (Mirza Hoseyn-'Ali Nuri), Iranian founder of Bahá'í faith (shown, its center in Delhi, India), declares that he's the messenger of God. Prophesied by the Bab, a 19th- century Shi'ite prophet, he's regarded as the savior whose mission is to heal the discord between religions and establish a universal world religion, as all religions are manifestations of God. The central focus of Bahá'í faith is the unity of mankind; the religion has no formal priesthood or sacraments. Rather, believers pray daily, practice an ethical way of life, and engage in observances such as a communal 19-day fast, similar to the Islamic Ramadan. The teachings of Bahá'u'lláh are contained in the holy scripture, the Kitab-i-Iqan.

1865 William Booth founds Salvation Army in London, a Protestant evangelical denomination and charitable institution. Booth, a Methodist minister, founds missions in the slums of London to help society's disadvantaged. In 1878, the name Salvation Army is officially adopted and the organization is structured according to a military model with hierarchical ranks of officers. Worship services are informal and don't include sacraments, and instead encompass prayer, music, and personal testimony. The Salvation Army now has branches in over 110 countries.

1866 Mary Baker Eddy (Mary Baker Glover by her first marraige), founder of the Christian Science movement, allegedly cures her injuries from a fall by reading the New Testament. Eddy, raised Congregationalist with little formal education, is plagued by health problems through her adult life and experiments with homeopathy and mental healing methods. After her spiritual healing, she develops her teaching that illness is an illusion that can be healed by knowing God. She publishes *Science and Health with Key to the Scriptures* in 1875, containing the main principles of her thought. She founds the Church of Christ, Scientist in Boston in 1879. In 1908, at the age of 87, she founds the *Christian Science Monitor*.

1868 State Shinto, as the official nationalistic religion, flourishes in Japan from the Meiji Restoration period (1868–1912) until the end of World War II. A response to modernization and Western colonial powers, it represents a movement to reaffirm the centrality of the emperor in Japanese society by promoting emperor worship. It's promoted in the schools and other government institutions until it's abolished in 1945 as a condition of Japanese surrender to the Allied forces.

1869 The First Vatican Council is convened by Pope Pius IX. The Council approves a definition of the Pope's authority that includes infallibility on doctrinal matters.

1875 Russian-born mystic Helena Petrova Blavatsky (Madam Blavatsky) founds the Theosophical Society with Henry S. Olcott in New York. Its stated mission is the creation of a universal fellowship of humanity; the study of the great scriptures of world religions, philosophy, and science; and the investigation of the mysteries of nature and the spiritual powers of human beings. Theosophical Society headquarters are moved to India in 1879, and in 1888 Blavatsky's most famous work, *The Secret Doctrine*, is published.

1875

1886 Death of Ramakrishna Paramahamsa, one of the most famous saints of Vedanta Hinduism. As a young man, Ramakrishna prays to Goddess Kali; downcast that she hasn't answered his prayers, he attempts suicide and, at that moment, is overcome with divine bliss. He goes on to pursue spiritual truths of all religions, becoming convinced that the ultimate consciousness of Brahman is to be found in all faiths. His message gains popularity in British-ruled India and he gathers disciples. Upon his death, his disciple Swami Vivekananda takes over leadership of the community and formally establishes the Ramakrishna Order, which is instrumental in spreading Hindu teachings to the West.

1889 Native American mystic Wovoka, a Northern Paiute from Nevada, has a vision during an eclipse in which he speaks to God and is charged with teaching the Ghost Dance in order to spread the message that the dead will come back to life. The Ghost Dance, which combines traditional religion with Christianity, is a short-lived millennial movement among Western Native American tribes that prophesies the restoration of traditional culture and the end of white occupation through a communal dance lasting several days. Wovoka is said to display stigmata and is widely regarded as a Messiah for the Indians. The dance spreads among Western tribes and tragically, is practiced by the Sioux just before their massacre at Wounded Knee, South Dakota.

1893 Parliament of the World's Religions takes place in Chicago. The Parliament, lasting over two weeks, is the first formal gathering of religious leaders from Eastern and Western spiritual traditions. One highlight is the address by Swami Vivekananda of the Ramakrishna Order, introducing Hinduism to many in the Western world. The Parliament is regarded as the beginning of worldwide interfaith dialogue.

Contemporary Religion: The 20th Century and Beyond

With the dawn of the twentieth century, the forces of modernization continued to accelerate, having a defining impact on religion. As the globe shrank due to the increasing speed of travel and communications technology, economic and political decentralization followed, leading to mass migrations of populations and the weakening of the traditional nation-state with its well-defined borders. Increasing cultural pluralism and the predominance of science continued to supplant traditional religious worldviews, leading to an ever more secular culture. In the face of these daunting pressures, a variety of religious and spiritual responses emerged, often led by those marginalized by the changes in mainstream society. Among these responses were a trio of interrelated phenomena that we find woven throughout this era: New Religious Movements, fundamentalism, and millennialism.

Scholars have a special name for the new religions often popularly termed "cults": New Religious Movements. These groups, arising outside the accepted forms of established religions, vary widely, but tend to share certain characteristics. In their extreme form, these groups sometimes commit acts of mass violence, driven by their religious ideology. In recent years, the media covered such events as the arrest and deportation of Indian guru Bhagwan Shree Rajneesh following crimes at his Oregon ranch, the murders at the Waco, Texas,

compound of the Branch Davidians headed by David Koresh, and the group suicide of the UFO cult Heavens' Gate. Internationally, this trend is borne out by the Tokyo subway gassings of the Aum Shinrikyo group. Though these events make a great impact on popular consciousness, such violent incidents are relatively rare. Less extreme are numerous groups which, though outside the mainstream, have not committed acts of mass violence, such as Scientology and the Chinese group Falun Gong.

Fundamentalism can likewise be understood as a response to the pressures of modernity. The particular forms it takes are numerous and can be found in religions as diverse as Christianity, Islam, Buddhism, and Hinduism. Nevertheless, fundamentalism has an identifiable set of characteristics. Fundamentalists see their efforts as a noble fight for survival, often construed as a war between good and evil of apocalyptic proportions, waged on the battleground of culture and politics. They focus on key doctrines and traditional practices in order to affirm their threatened identity. Their ultimate goal is to win the battle for the sacred in a world they see as devoid of spiritual values. Fundamentalism finds its extreme expression in terrorism, which brings religious and ideological convictions onto the political plane.

Millennialism is a related theme which, though found in religions from the early periods of history, has had a particularly volatile reemergence in recent times. Derived from the biblical notion in the Book of Revelation that, prior to the Last Judgment, Christ will preside over a thousand-year reign of peace (the millennium), the term denotes a more general trend found in many world religions, including Judaism, Buddhism, and Hinduism, as well as in many recent sects. It is expressed in themes of the impending apocalypse and a radical overturning of the present corrupt system to form a new world order. Because of its potentially revolutionary message, such groups are often threatening to current power structures.

These themes played out in a series of dramatic political and cultural events that crossed the world stage. Against the backdrop of two world wars culminating in the advent of the nuclear age with the detonation of the atom bomb, events transpired that irrevocably changed the world in which we live.

During this period, a series of thinkers, theologians, and humanitarians offered their visions for solving man's problems and understanding his soul, creating new concepts to address the unprecedented perils and potentials of the new era. Among these were the humanitarian and doctor Albert Schweitzer; the father of psychoanalysis, Sigmund Freud (who attributed religious experience to unconscious drives); the influential theologians Martin Buber, Thomas Merton, and Paul Tillich; and the Catholic luminary Mother Teresa.

The encounter between East and West that began in the previous three centuries has continued at an accelerated pace as the era of European colonial power ended. Events in India, notably the struggle for independence and the partition of India and Pakistan, produced a group of great thinkers, among them the mystic Sri Aurobindo, the poet Rabindranath Tagore, the Buddhist populist leader B. R. Ambedkar, and most famously, Mahatma Gandhi. Meanwhile, Indian teachers of yoga and Buddhist and Hindu philosophy came to America and Europe as emissaries: Krishnamurti, Yogananda, Maharishi Mahesh Yogi, as well as the Dalai Lama. From the Far East, such figures as Japanese Buddhist teacher D. T. Suzuki explained Zen philosophy to Western audiences.

In America, the civil rights movement marked the latter half of the twentieth century. Martin Luther King Jr, Malcolm X, and, more recently, the Million Man March of Louis Farrakhan led the nation toward equality, often in the context of an appeal to religious ethics. Churches served as the womb of the movement, mobilizing a wide grass-roots campaign that overturned the repressive policies of the past and helped to fade the legacy of slavery. Gradually, the movement's ideals have extended to include other minorities, women, and the gay community but the struggle continues, as recent debates over ordination of gay and female clergy and gay marriage show.

Lastly, the current era is marked by the global rise of Islam, the fastest-growing religion worldwide. The next decades will be defined largely by the cultural encounter between the rising Islamic world and the West. It will depend on our collective powers of tolerance and mutual understanding whether this development results in escalating episodes of mass violence, or in a new cultural Renaissance honoring the achievements of all traditions.

1901 Rabindranath Tagore, Bengali poet, writer, and artist, founds Shantiniketan ("Abode of Peace"), an experimental school in rural Bengal that combines Indian and Western artistic traditions. Son of influential religious reformer Debendranath Tagore, he's educated in both India and England and distinguishes himself with his poetry, which addresses themes of spirituality and social injustice. In 1913 he's awarded the Nobel Prize for Literature for his *Gitanjali, Song Offerings*. Highly influential in bridging Indian and Western cultures, he's widely regarded as India's most eminent poet.

1908 Sri Aurobindo, Indian mystic and nationalist, has a spiritual conversion. A freedom fighter for Indian independence in his youth, he has a vision while contemplating the Bhagavad Gita in prison, in which he sees his jailers as manifestations of Vishnu (God) and henceforth devotes his life to spiritual truth. Settling in Pondicherry in Southern India, he founds an ashram, and later the utopian city of Auroville (shown, Matrimandir, the main temple

there). In 1920 he meets Mirra Richard, known as the Mother, who becomes his spiritual counterpart. Aurobindo's teachings focus on the evolutionary movement of spiritual consciousness called Supramental Truth, based on the teachings of Vedanta philosophy and yoga. He writes many books, including *The Life Divine* and the *Synthesis of Yoga*.

1900

1906 Albert Schweitzer, German theologian and physician, writes the *Quest for the Historical Jesus*, which emphasizes the apocalyptic beliefs of Jesus and Paul. A man of diverse talent, he studies medicine, is an accomplished musician, and writes widely in theology and philosophy, stressing reverence for life as a fundamental ethical principle. Wishing to devote himself to humanitarian causes, he travels to Africa in 1913 to become a mission doctor. He founds a hospital at Lambaréné in French Equatorial Africa and treats thousands of patients, many with leprosy. He's awarded the 1952 Nobel Peace Prize for his efforts.

1913 Sigmund Freud publishes *Totem and Taboo*, the first of several works attempting to apply his psychoanalytic theory to culture. In these works he discusses such concepts as primitive urges, cultural taboos, guilt, totems, and myths in an attempt to explain the origin of religion. Though highly speculative, Freud's ideas have had great impact on theories of culture and religion. His other related works are *Civilization and Its Discontents* and *The Future of an Illusion*.

1917 Following World War I, Palestine, including Jerusalem, comes under British control. In 1920 the League of Nations assigns the Mandate of Palestine to Britain, which lasts until 1948.

90

1919 "Vailala Madness," first widely recognized incident of cargo cult practice, occurs in Papua New Guinea. Cargo cults arise in Melanesia in colonial settings and are mass apocalyptic movements centered around charismatic "prophets" who foretell a new age heralded by the arrival of divine "cargo" by plane or ship. Cargo, or Western goods, are thought to be divinely created and unfairly controlled by white people. Because of the revolutionary nature of these cults, believing that the positions of whites and natives should be reversed, they are typically suppressed by authorities.

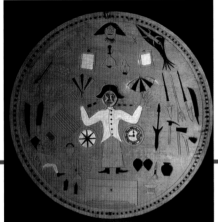

1923 German Jewish theologian Martin Buber publishes his masterpiece, *I and Thou*. Buber, who later fled the Nazi regime for Palestine, is a leading Jewish intellectual who holds many influential academic posts and advocates Arab-Israeli cooperation in the formation of the Jewish state. His theological thought is marked by the emphasis on the mutual relationship between man and God, which serves as the model for human relationships.

1920 The Self-Realization Fellowship of Paramahansa Yogananda, Hindu teacher of yoga, is established in Los Angeles. One of the first Indian spiritual teachers to take up residence in the West, Yogananda teaches the practice of Kriya Yoga, which proclaims that the illusion of material bondage can be transcended through self-knowledge. In 1946 his book *Autobiography of a Yogi* is published, and becomes a spiritual classic. Upon Yogananda's death, some of his followers claim that his body does not decay.

1925 The "Scopes Monkey Trial" begins, in which John Scopes is accused of teaching evolution in his high school biology classroom in violation of the newly passed Butler Act. Prosecutor William Jennings Bryan, a political candidate and Christian fundamentalist, and defense attorney Clarence Darrow engage in a much-publicized debate (the first U.S. trial to be broadcast on national radio) in which Bryan is largely discredited for his literal reading of the biblical account of creation. Still, the jury finds Scopes technically guilty and fines him $100. The case is appealed and the conviction overturned on a technicality. The Butler Act is not overturned until 1968.

1925 Adolf Hitler publishes the first volume of his autobiography, *Mein Kampf* (*My Struggle*), written during his imprisonment in Landsberg. It contains elements of his political ideology that will become central to the rise of the Nazi party during World War II: the doctrine of supremacy

of the "Aryan" race and anti-Semitism. Hitler draws on many sources, such as the racial supremacist theories of Houston Stewart Chamberlain, the philosophy of Friedrich Nietzsche, and the mythic themes of Wagnerian opera.

1929 Jiddu Krishnamurti, Indian philosopher and religious leader, declares independence from Theosophical movement. As a boy, Krishnamurti is recognized by Theosophical leaders C. W. Leadbeater and Annie Besantas the prophesied World Teacher and is raised to fulfill that role. Disillusioned after the death of his brother, Krishnamurti rejects this identity and begins a career as an independent spiritual teacher, becoming well known in the West and giving many talks later compiled into publications by his followers. He opposes the formation of religious institutions and is known for his view that "truth is a pathless land" which cannot be approached by any particular creed. In 1984 he's awarded the UN Peace Medal.

1930

1928 Spanish priest Josemaria Escriva de Balaguer y Albas founds a Roman Catholic organization of laymen and clergy called Opus Dei. The

organization gains the approval of the Papacy and in 1982 is established as a personal prelature of the Church by John Paul II. The majority of members are supernumeraries, usually families who, in their everyday lives, are dedicated to implementing Christian values in society. Popularized in the *Da Vinci Code* by Dan Brown, the portrayal of the organization in the book is generally considered inaccurate. Escriva (his tomb in the Vatican, shown) was canonized in 2002.

1930 Mohandas Gandhi (known as Mahatma, "Great Soul") leader of the Indian Independence movement and pioneer of civil disobedience, leads protesters in the nearly 240-mile Dandi Salt March from March 12 to April 6 to protest British salt tax. At the seaside, protestors symbolically make their own salt. The march results in the imprisonment of tens of thousands.

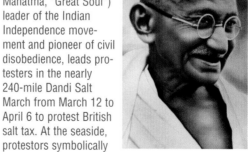

The Great Soul of Mahatma Gandhi

Born in 1869 to an observant Vaisnava Hindu household, Mohandas K. Gandhi is educated as a lawyer in England and begins his career in South Africa, where he becomes involved in the struggle for equal rights for Indians. Continuing his political activities in India, he advocates a policy of nonviolent resistance to British rule—known as Satyagraha ("effort at Truth") based on the principle of ahimsa (nonviolence) inspired by his understanding of Hinduism and other religions—and spends much time in prison for his antigovernment actions. In 1947 he's instrumental in negotiating India's formal independence from Britain, and in January, 1948, he's killed by an assassin. Gandhi is a lifelong devotee of the Bhagavad Gita and its message of spiritual nonattachment and devotion to truth. He's also influenced by Christian and Muslim scriptures and promotes the idea that all religions are expressions of one Truth. His spiritual convictions are the source of great inner strength that allows him to endure many hardships in the struggle for freedom.

1930   Mining engineer Guy Ballard allegedly meets Ascended Master St. Germain (pictured) on Mt. Shasta, California. After St. Germain reveals Ballard's past lives and the plan for evolution on earth, Ballard starts the I AM movement with wife, Edna, the two acting as channels for the Ascended Masters, including St. Germain and Jesus. At its peak in the late 1930s, the movement has several million followers nationwide. However, the Ballards are accused of fraud, and many followers leave the movement after Guy's death, which belies his claim of immortality. The I AM movement is still active on a smaller scale today.

1930   Founding of Soka Gakkai, Japanese Buddhist organization based on Nichiren Buddhism. Originally called Soka Kyoiku Gakkai (Value-Creation Education Society), it's founded by Tsunesaburo Makiguchi and renamed Soka Gakkai in 1946 by Josei Toda. In 1975 Soka Gakkai International is founded, containing branches in over 190 countries and over 12 million members. As with all schools of Nichiren Buddhism, Soka Gakkai focuses on the study and worship of the Lotus Sutra, and the chant *Nam-myoho-renge-kyo* (Hail to the Lotus Sutra) remains a central practice of the group. Closely affiliated with the New Komeito political party which enjoys great influence in Japan, Soka Gakkai has been criticized for its aggressive proselytizing and alleged harassment of members who leave the organization. In 1992 Soka Gakkai is excommunicated by the high priest of Nichiren Shoshu in Japan.

1930   The Rastafarian movement starts among the Jamaican working class, black population and takes its name from Ras (Prince) Tafari Makonnen, the former name of emperor of Ethiopia, Haile Selassie I. Known by biblical titles such as the "Lion of Judah," he is coronated on November 2, and is regarded as the Messiah, an incarnation of God. In the following years, several Jamaican prophets express the view that blacks are the Israelites reincarnated and have endured oppression at the hands of whites as punishment for their sins; led by Ras Tafari, they will return to Africa as their Holy Land.

Rastafarianism

The Rastafarian movement reflects a rejection of Western culture and values known as Babylon and a dedication to the idea of Zion, representing the true kingdom of God or Jah (from Jehovah). Many Rastafarians practice a largely vegetarian diet inspired by Biblical dietary laws and champion qualities seen as antithetical to Western civilization, such as wearing uncombed hair or dreadlocks and smoking *ganja* or marijuana. The movement is spread worldwide by the popularity of Reggae music, especially in the figure of musician Bob Marley who combines elements of religion and political activism typical of Rastafarianism.

Gnostic Gospels

The Nag Hammadi texts have a revolutionary impact on Biblical scholarship and change the understanding of early Christianity. Before their discovery, virtually all that was known about Gnosticism was from Christian sources, which portrayed it in a negative light. The Nag Hammadi texts suggest that in the early centuries after Christ there were many sects considering themselves Christian but having widely differing understandings of the nature of Christ and the role of Church authority and sacraments. The Gnostic approach focuses on individual mystic insight as opposed to institutionally sanctioned sacraments and the dogma of the Church, emphasizing that the truth which confers spiritual immortality resides within oneself. The most famous of the collection is perhaps the Gospel of Thomas, which, according to Willis Barnstone's *The Other Bible: Ancient Alternative Scriptures*, begins with the words "These are the secret sayings which the living Jesus spoke and which Didymos Judas Thomas wrote down." Other texts in the corpus include *The Gospel of Truth* and *The Thunder, Perfect Mind*.

1945 Discovery of the *Nag Hammadi* Scriptures (Gnostic Gospels) in Northern Egypt by local villagers who happen upon buried jars containing 13 papyrus codices in Coptic Egyptian dating from around the 4th century (though the original texts probably date from the 2nd century). The manuscripts contain 52 texts, mostly Gnostic, and are thought to have been hidden by monks from nearby monastery of St. Pachomius when these texts were banned by the Church as heretical.

1945

1945 At the end of World War II, a condition of Japanese surrender to the Allied Powers is the dismantling of all State Shinto shrines, known as "disestablishment," and the renunciation by the emperor of his claim to be a living god. Shinto practices continue in a secular context.

1945 German Protestant theologian Dietrich Bonhoeffer is executed by the Nazis for his participation in a plot to overthrow Adolf Hitler. He's active in the Confessing Church, a Protestant resistance movement to the Nazi regime, when his undercover activities are discovered by the Nazis, leading to his imprisonment.

1947 Indian Independence from British rule and Partition, which separates the Muslim majority state of Pakistan in the northeast from the predominantly Hindu territory of the remainder of India. In the population transfer of millions across borders, large-scale riots and chaos result in hundreds of thousands of Hindu and Muslim deaths.

1947 On November 29, the United Nations Partition Plan for Palestine calls for the creation of separate Jewish and Arab states, ending the British Mandate of Palestine. Jerusalem is to be placed under international administration, but the majority of Arabs object to this plan, while the majority of Jews are in favor of it, leading to the Arab-Israeli War of 1948.

1947 Earliest discovery of the Dead Sea Scrolls. Comprising over 800 fragmentary Aramaic and Hebrew manuscripts on papyrus and parchment, the scrolls are found largely in 11 caves around the ruins of the ancient settlement of Khirbet Qumran, widely believed to be a community of the Jewish Essenes, an esoteric sect that split off from the Jewish mainstream in the 2nd century B.C. over a dispute with the Maccabean priesthood of Jerusalem. Discovery of manuscripts continues until 1956.

1948 American Trappist monk, writer and mystic, Thomas Merton publishes his book *Seven Storey Mountain*, which gains great recognition. The book is autobiographical and contains his private spiritual reflections. As a young man, Merton converts to Catholicism and later joins the Trappist Abby of Gethsemani in Kentucky, where he dedicates himself to the Order's rule of silence, contemplation, and seclusion. Later, Merton becomes vocal in his objection to the Vietnam War and active in promoting interfaith dialogue. He travels widely in Asia, meeting with such figures as the Dalai Lama, and his later works reflect a profound understanding of Eastern traditions. His writings—over 50 books—are published after his death. Among them, his diaries gain great recognition as spiritual classics.

1950 Ramana Maharshi, Indian yogi and guru of Advaita Vedanta, dies. Born Venkataraman Aiyer to a Brahmin family in South India, he's drawn to writings of the Indian mystics as a boy, and at age 17 has a defining spiritual experience of the fear of death. This leads to a deep self-questioning of "who am I" culminating in the realization that the indwelling spirit is deathless and eternal. Attaining *samādhi*, the bliss of enlightenment, Ramana Maharshi leaves home to live as a hermit on Mount Arunachala, a traditional holy site, where he remains for the rest of his life in silent contemplation. Famous for his teaching of *ātma-vicāra*, or self-inquiry, Ramana Maharshi becomes an influential transmitter of the Vedantic tradition of Hinduism to the West.

1950

1950 Guru and miracle-worker Sathya Sai Baba establishes an ashram in India. Sathya begins performing miracles as a young boy and identifies himself as the reincarnation of spiritual master Shirdi Sai Baba, gaining many followers. He teaches the principles of truth, right conduct, peace, love, non-violence, and the unity of all world religions. He becomes famous worldwide for his manifestation of "miracles" such as the apparent materialization of objects such as watches and jewelry and the sacred ash called *vibhuti*. With millions of followers worldwide, his organization has sponsored many charitable works, including schools, hospitals and public service projects in India.

1950 World Fellowship of Buddhists is founded in Colombo, Sri Lanka, to represent Buddhists worldwide. It's the largest Buddhist organization, representing over 27 countries from all schools of Buddhism.

1951 Daisetsu Teitaro (D. T.) Suzuki, Japanese Zen Buddhist scholar and teacher, tours American universities. Suzuki, a disciple of famous Zen master Sōen Shaku, attains *satori*, or enlightenment, and spends much of his later life in the West teaching and writing. He does much to introduce Westerners to Zen Buddhism, founding the Eastern Buddhist Society, and serving as professor at Columbia University for a number of years, in addition to his professorship at Otani University in Japan. He writes several influential books, including *Essays in Zen Buddhism*.

Scientology

The Church of Scientology teaches what it views as a method by which to heal conditions such as addictions, mental illness, and cancer. It presents a step-by-step process by which a person, known as a *thetan* (an immortal spiritual being), gradually frees himself of physical and mental impurities (known as *engrams* or implants), including the effects of drugs and the imprints of traumas from childhood or past lives. One eventually reaches the stage of Clear, then a kind of enlightenment called Operating Thetan. The group has come under criticism by mainstream religions, governments, and anticult groups for its secretive practices and aggressive response to critics.

1952 Paul Tillich, German-American Protestant theologian, publishes *The Courage to Be*. A Lutheran clergyman and professor in Germany, he's openly critical of the Nazi movement, leading to his emigration to America, where he teaches at Union Theological Seminary, Harvard University, and the University of Chicago. Tillich's thought combines existentialist philosophy with Protestant principles, seeking to reconcile faith with human experience and culture. His other influential works include *Dynamics of Faith* and *Faith and Systematic Theology*.

1952 Science-fiction author L. Ron Hubbard starts a New Religious Movement originally called Dianetics, later changed to the Church of Scientology. The group has gained much attention due to its celebrity members such as John Travolta and Tom Cruise. Estimates of membership vary from several hundred thousand to several million worldwide.

1955 Pierre Teilhard de Chardin, French Jesuit priest, theologian and paleontologist, dies. His major works, including *The Divine Milieu* and *The Phenomenon of Man*, are forbidden by the Jesuits to be published during his life. After serving in WWI, and teaching in Paris, Teilhard embarks on a paleontological expedition in China, where he spends the next two decades and is involved in the discovery of the skull of Peking man in 1929. Blending his modern science with Christian faith, Teilhard develops the view that man is evolving toward the Omega Point, a final unity that represents the realization of Christ.

1959 China invades Western Tibet and destroys most Buddhist monasteries. The Dalai Lama, religious and secular leader of Tibet, flees to India with 100,000 Tibetan refugees. Tibetan Government-in-exile is established in India.

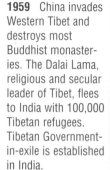

1956 Untouchable (or *Dalit,* the lowest Hindu social class, literally outside of the caste system) leader B. R. Ambedkar (shown, background poster) renounces Hinduism and converts, along with more than 200,000 *Dalit* followers, to Buddhism, beginning the modern neo-Buddhist movement. Born to a *Dalit* family, Ambedkar is educated in America and England as a lawyer and enters government service in India. Sensitive to the discrimination he faces, he becomes a leader in the cause of rights for low-caste peoples. In 1947 he becomes Minister for Law of India, helping to frame the Indian constitution which outlaws discrimination against *Dalits.* Along with such figures as Gandhi, he's one of the fathers of Indian independence.

1959 Maharishi Mahesh Yogi, founder of Transcendental Meditation, makes his first tour of the West. Practicing under his guru in the Himalayas for years, Maharishi establishes an ashram in Northern India near the Ganges and begins to teach his method of meditation, which involves the repetition of a mantra or sacred phrase. Maharishi is made famous by the Beatles, who become his students, along with other celebrities such as the Beach Boys. He has published numerous books, has an online university, and many teaching centers, claiming millions of followers worldwide.

1959 Sri Lankan Prime Minister S.W.R.D. Bandaranaike is assassinated by Buddhist monk Talduwe Somarama, shot while prostrate in the traditional Buddhist greeting. He's killed as part of a conspiracy by an antigovernment Buddhist faction. Somarama is found guilty and converts to Christianity shortly before his execution.

1960

1962–1965 Second Vatican Council, the 21st ecumenical council, is opened by Pope John XXIII and closed by Pope Paul VI. Called in order to address the challenges of the church in the modern era, the tone of the Council tends toward a liberal approach. Among the documents approved are those acknowledging legitimate sources of sanctity outside the Church, the innocence of Jews from responsibility for the death of Christ, and the revision of the liturgy to incorporate vernacular language, rather than Latin alone, making it more accessible to lay people.

1963 Rev. Dr. Martin Luther King Jr. (1929–1968), Baptist minister and civil rights leader, delivers his famous "I Have a Dream" speech to a crowd of over 250,000 during the March on Washington for Jobs and Freedom in Washington, D.C. King was born in Atlanta, Georgia, received his education at Morehouse College, Crozer Theological Seminary, and Boston University.

Martin Luther King Jr.

Dr. Martin Luther King Jr., pastor of the Dexter Avenue Baptist Church in Montgomery, Alabama, enters the Civil Rights movement leading to the Montgomery Bus Boycott in 1955. The Boycott lasts 381 days, unleashing tensions resulting in the bombing of King's house and his arrest, and ultimately leads to a U.S. Supreme Court decision outlawing racial segregation on all public transportation.

King continues his civil rights work, influenced by the philosophy of Mahatma Gandhi, which advocated nonviolent civil disobedience. He is integral in founding in 1957 the Southern Christian Leadership Conference (SCLC) which organizes black churches to engage in nonviolent protests. The success of the Civil Rights movement leads to the passing into United States law the Civil Rights Act of 1964, and the Voting Rights Act of 1965. In 1964 King is awarded the Nobel Prize for Peace.

On April 4, 1968, King is assassinated. A crowd of 300,000 attends his funeral. Posthumously, King is awarded the Presidential Medal of Freedom (1977) and the Congressional Gold Medal (2004). In 1986 Martin Luther King Day is established as a national holiday.

1965 On February 21, Malcolm X, African-American leader and converted Muslim, is assassinated by 3 Black Muslims while speaking in Harlem, New York City. Approximately 1600 people attend his funeral in Harlem.

The Evolving View of Malcolm X

Malcolm X is born Malcolm Little in Omaha, Nebraska. After a tough youth in which he engages in petty crime, he's sentenced to prison, where he converts to the Nation of Islam, a black militant nationalist group headed by Elijah Muhammad. On his release, he rises to second in command of the group, founding many Muslim temples and becoming a vocal spokesperson for black separatism and use of violence in self-defense, which causes him to be watched by the FBI and rejected by mainstream civil rights activists. In 1964 he makes a traditional pilgrimage to Mecca and has a change of heart, as he sees many races united under Islam. He returns to the U.S. a mainstream Sunni Muslim with a more tolerant attitude towards race relations. However, tensions mount between him and Nation of Islam leaders and the plot to assassinate him is formed.

1967 The Six-Day War is initiated by Israel against Egypt and other Arab nations after growing tension caused by a series of hostile moves by Egypt, including the blocking of sea routes and deploy-

ment of armed forces near Israeli border. Israel gains control of Gaza Strip, Sinai Peninsula, West Bank, and Golan Heights, territories that are disputed today.

1970

1971 The Unification Church of Rev. Sun Myung Moon shifts its base to New York. Founded in 1954 in South Korea, church doctrine holds that Moon is the Messiah, charged with the mission to complete Jesus' work of restoring the Kingdom of God on Earth. Moon also believes that Jesus' mission, which should have culminated in marriage and family, was interrupted by his crucifixion. Moon and his wife, Hak Ja Han, thus represent the male and female aspects of the Messiah. A central aspect of the group's beliefs focus on devotion to marriage and family, and Moon gains notoriety in the West for his mass marriage ceremonies. The group, which has several hundred thousand followers in over 100 countries, has been accused of cultlike practices, including aggressive recruiting, brainwashing tactics, and financial solicitation.

New Religious Movements

Scholars use the term "New Religious Movement" (NRM) to refer to what is often popularly termed a "cult." NRMs are relatively recent religious or spiritual groups that are not established forms of the major world religions. These groups, though differing widely in terms of belief and practice, have in common a "family resemblance": a group bonded together against the unique pressures and circumstances of modernity—the rise of secularism and technology, the increasing focus on the individual, and the high rate of social change. Characteristics of NRMs include: the combination of elements from different traditions; the view that the group is outside of mainstream society, which is often regarded as corrupt; and the presence of a charismatic founder who is often regarded as possessing special powers. Many "New Age" groups fall within this category, and the phenomenon of "channeling" spiritual entities, as well as apocalyptic beliefs, are elements that occur widely in NRMs.

1971 Bangladesh is formed from a portion of West Pakistan as a country of Bengali Muslims. Designated East Pakistan at the time of Indian Partition in 1947, a cultural and linguistic divide exists between the two Muslim regions, which generates increasing tension, finally resulting in the bloody Bangladesh Liberation War, causing hundreds of thousands of deaths and millions of refugees.

1972 The first openly gay person to be ordained in any Christian organization is Rev. William Johnson, of the United Church of Christ in San Francisco. The same year Sally Priesand (shown) of Reform Judaism becomes the first woman to be ordained as a rabbi.

1973–84 Eighth-century Buddhist monument Borobudur is restored by UNESCO and Indonesian Archaeological Service. It's the largest Buddhist monument on earth.

1975–79 Under Pol Pot, leader of the Khmer Rouge, Cambodian Communists attempt to eradicate Buddhism, killing and exiling almost all Buddhist monks and intellectuals, and destroying every Buddhist temple and library. Estimates of the dead range from 1 to 3 million people.

1978 Pope John Paul II takes office. The only Polish Pope, his reign, lasting over 26 years, is characterized by his outspoken opposition to communism, his extensive travel to numerous countries including those in Latin America, Africa, and India, and his emphasis on traditional Catholic doctrine that prohibits contraception and abortion and mandates priestly celibacy and exclusively male ordination. He's an extremely popular Pope, drawing millions to his public appearances worldwide.

1976 The Episcopal church approves the ordination of women as priests and bishops. The first Episcopal woman bishop is Barbara Clementine Harris, who was ordained in Massachusetts in 1989.

1979 Ayatollah Khomeini, Shi'ite Muslim leader of the Iranian Revolution, comes to power, establishing the first Muslim government in the world in over 50 years. Under his rule, from November 4, 1979, to January 20, 1981 —a period of 444 days—52 American hostages are held in the U.S. embassy in Tehran.

1980

1981 Indian guru Bhagwan Shree Rajneesh, a.k.a. Osho, founds Rajneeshpuram, a spiritual community of several thousand in Oregon. His teachings are an eclectic mix of spiritual traditions, such as Hinduism, Buddhism, and Zen, focusing on individual liberation from conceptual mind and social mores. He attracts much notoriety for his promotion of sexual freedom, and growing problems plague the Oregon ashram; accusations of attempted murder, bio-terrorism, and vote fraud are made and Rajneesh's lavish lifestyle, including his famous 93 Rolls-Royces, such as shown, come under criticism. In 1985 Rajneesh is deported on charges of immigration fraud and returns to India. In 1989 he takes the Zen Buddhist title Osho and continues to teach until his death in 1990.

1985 Jesus Seminar founded by biblical scholar Robert Funk under the auspices of the Westar Institute. The mission of the Seminar is to determine the degree to which the biblical accounts of Jesus' teachings and life are historical fact, rather than tradition. The Seminar contains about 100 members, who meet semi-annually to vote on the findings of research, using a coded system of colored beads to arrive at a consensual decision. Their

findings emphasize Jesus as a human wisdom teacher, rather than a divine incarnation, and reflect the Seminar's intent to demythologize the Jesus story. The findings and methods of the Seminar have been widely publicized and have drawn criticism from more traditional Christian scholars.

1984 Desmond Tutu, South African cleric and political activist, is awarded Nobel Peace Prize for his work against apartheid. During his career, Tutu is named the first black Anglican archbishop of Cape Town and primate of the Church of the Province of South Africa. Holding a variety of clerical posts in Africa and the UK, Tutu is active in the struggle for black civil rights. From the time of the 1976 Soweto Riots, a mass uprising against apartheid, Tutu supported an economic boycott against the government. After the end of apartheid in the early 1990s, he heads the Truth and Reconciliation Commission, a judicial body formed to redress the wrongs against victims of apartheid.

1989 Dalai Lama awarded Nobel Peace Prize for his nonviolent resistance to Chinese occupation of Tibet.

Burmese Buddhist Activist Aung San Suu Kyi

Aung San Suu Kyi enters politics in 1988 as a new military regime is taking power and mass demonstrations for democracy are being violently suppressed. She founds the National League for Democracy, inspired by Mahatma Gandhi's philosophy of nonviolence, and is placed under house arrest by the military regime after refusing to leave the country. In 1990 her party wins the majority vote, making her the rightful Prime Minister elect, but the military regime refuses to step down. Using her position as an opportunity to speak for human rights and democracy, she's a mouthpiece for Burmese independence (she prefers the name Burma to Myanmar), drawing on Buddhist principles to articulate a philosophy of nonviolent social engagement.

1991 Burmese Buddhist leader Aung San Suu Kyi wins Nobel Peace Prize for her nonviolent efforts for democracy against the repressive military regime in Myanmar.

1990

1993 On April 19, after a 51 day siege, the FBI and Bureau of Alcohol, Tobacco and Firearms (ATF) raid the Branch Davidian compound at Waco, Texas. The resulting fire kills over 70 people, including 17 children and Davidian leader David Koresh. Allegations of weapons possession spurred the raid, but Koresh is also accused of child abuse, polygamy, and of fathering numerous children by the group's underage female members. Many of the Branch Davidians believe that Koresh is a Messiah who will return at a future date.

1989 Iranian leader Ayatollah Khomeini issues a *fatwah* calling for the assassination of British author Salman Rushdie for "blasphemous" depiction of Prophet Muhammad in his book *The Satanic Verses*, offering a $3 million bounty. Rushdie goes into hiding under the protection of British security forces.

1992 On December 6, riots break out after members of the Hindu fundamentalist Bharatia Janata Party destroy the Islamic Babri Mosque at Ayodhya, a site also holy to Hindus as the birthplace of god Ram of the *Ramayana*. The violence spreads throughout India, sparking simmering Hindu-Muslim tensions, resulting in widespread looting and violence with a death toll over 1,000.

1994 Taliban fundamentalists, headed by Mullah Mohammed Omar, begin their rise to power in Afghanistan. Over the next few years this Sunni Islamist nationalist movement seizes control of most of Afghanistan and implements rule by *shari'a*, or Islamic law, which includes strict punishments such as stoning or amputation of a limb for crimes such as adultery and theft. Music, televi-sion, and alcohol are prohibited. Men are required to wear beards; women are required to wear the burqa, or full-body veil.

1995 Aum Shinrikyo, a New Religious Movement founded by charismatic leader Shoko Asahara in 1984, releases poison gas in the subway in Tokyo, Japan; 12 die and thousands are injured. Asahara is tried and sentenced to death, and though it's unclear exactly why the attacks were initiated, it seems likely that it has to do with his apocalyptic beliefs. The movement combines elements of Hindu and Buddhist mysticism with the belief that an imminent series of disasters, including world war, will end the world and usher in a new cosmic era. In 2000 Aum Shinrikyo changes its name to Aleph and continues to operate, retaining many of its original beliefs and practices.

1995 On October 16, the Million Man March in Washington, D.C., takes place with estimates ranging from several hun-dred thousand to over 1 million participants. Louis Farrakhan, African-American leader of the Nation of Islam, is a prominent organizer of the march, and calls for black unity, political activism, and a commitment to tradi-tional family values. It's reported that voter registration among black men rises sharply after the event.

1996 American evangelist Billy Graham is awarded the Congressional Gold Medal. Ordained a Southern Baptist in 1939, Graham gains popularity for his persuasive preaching in large revival meetings, known as "crusades," and for his use of mass media, including radio, television, and Internet. He's an advisor to many U.S. presidents, starting with Harry Truman.

1997 Death of Mother Teresa (Agnes Gonxha Bojaxhiu), Roman Catholic nun from Macedonia, at the age of 87. During her life she founds the Missionaries of Charity, an order dedicated to serving the poor and destitute, originally of Calcutta, India. She's also the recipient of many awards and honors, and in 1979 she receives the Nobel Peace Prize. She is beatified by Pope John Paul II in 1993.

1998 President Khatami of Iran dissociates his government from Ayatollah Khomeini's *fatwah* against Salman Rushdie in the course of implementing cultural reforms such as a focus on democracy and greater rights for women.

1997 On March 23–25 members of the Heaven's Gate UFO cult in California commit mass suicide in preparation for the arrival of comet Hale-Bopp. The death toll is 39. Founders Marshall Applewhite and Bonnie Nettles' elaborate and seemingly delusional worldview centers on the notion that ascension to a higher level of evolution is imminent. Members believe themselves to be aliens in human bodies, and suicide at the time of the comet's approach is a way of casting off their human "vehicle" and joining the spaceship hidden behind it.

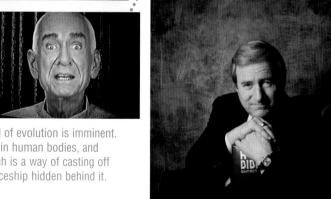

1999 Fundamentalist Baptist and televangelist preacher Jerry Falwell's newspaper, the *National Liberty Journal*, issues a "parental alert" warning that Tinky Winky, a character on the children's show *Teletubbies*, might be gay because of his purple color, "handbag," and the inverted triangle on his head.

New Religious Movement: Falun Gong

The Chinese neo-Taoist Movement Falun Gong, founded by Li Hongzhi in 1992, is based on a system of *ch'i-kung* meditation exercises and religious teachings that combine Buddhist and Taoist elements. It gains great popularity in China and later, abroad, with estimated membership of 70 to 100 million followers worldwide. Li Hongzhi, exiled from China, resides in America, and the group actively recruits members and protests Chinese government suppression. The group has been accused of being a "cult" by the Chinese government and questions have been raised about the group's financial and political practices. Popular religious movements have had a history of revolutionary activity in China, such as the famous Taiping Rebellion in the 19th century.

2000

1999 On July 20, Falun Gong (Practice of the Wheel of Law) also known as Falun Dafa (Great Law of the Wheel of Law) is officially suppressed by Chinese government after 10,000 members of the group engage in peaceful demonstration outside Chinese government building.

2000 The movie version of the *Left Behind* book series (beginning with *Left Behind: A Novel of the Earth's Last Days*) by Tim LaHaye and Jerry B. Jenkins is released on DVD and surprises Hollywood with its runaway sales before opening later in theatres. The movie stars Kirk Cameron and Chelsea Noble and centers on the apocalyptic Christian theme of the Rapture, whereby the faithful are taken up to heaven and those "left behind" on Earth witness the ominous events of the last days.

2001 On March 12, the Taliban blow up two 1,500-year-old Buddhist statues on the cliffs above Bamiyan, Afghanistan. Dating from the Gandharan period of Buddhist art, during which the area was a flourishing Buddhist center on the Silk Road, the figures were the largest standing Buddha statues in the world, rising about 120 feet high.

107

2001 On September 11, the World Trade Center and Pentagon are attacked by Muslim extremists identified as members of al-Qaeda. Almost 3,000 civilians die and the World Trade Center is destroyed.

2003 On December 10, Shirin Ebadi, Iranian judge and legal scholar, becomes the first Muslim woman and the first Iranian to win the Nobel Peace Prize. The award recognizes her contribution to human rights work, focusing especially on the rights of women and children.

2002 Pope John Paul II accepts the resignation of the archbishop of Boston, Bernard Cardinal Law. The scandal surrounding this event begins in Boston but quickly spreads to other Roman Catholic dioceses in America and concerns accusations that Cardinal Law covered up the sexual misconduct of priests in his jurisdiction. In an unprecedented action, over 50 priests sign a letter calling for his resignation. The Archdiocese of Boston looses millions of dollars in legal costs and is forced to close 65 parishes.

2003 On November 2, Gene Robinson, first openly gay bishop in Episcopal church, is ordained in New Hampshire.

2004 On February 25, Mel Gibson's film *The Passion of the Christ* is released and becomes the highest-grossing R-rated film ever. With dialogue in Aramaic, Latin, and Hebrew, and English subtitles, Gibson cowrites, coproduces, and directs the film, which reflects his Catholic views. Despite great success among Christian audiences, the film is considered controversial by many due to the graphic portrayals of Jesus' crucifixion and alleged anti-Semitic content.

2004 In April, candidates for the Sri Lankan political party Jaathika Hela Urumaya (National Heritage Party) led by Buddhist monks, win nine out of 225 seats in parliamentary elections, marking the clergy's entry into politics in this country.

2005 Death of Pope John Paul II on April 2. The funeral is attended by many heads of state. In an unprecedented gesture, memorials are observed by leaders from world religions, including Jewish, Muslim, and Christian Protestant and Eastern Orthodox denominations. Billions of people are believed to have watched the funeral on television.

2005 Pope Benedict XVI (Josef Ratzinger), a German, is elected to office on April 19 following the death of Pope John Paul II. He is the 265th Pope. Known as a conservative, he has stressed a return to fundamental Christian values.

Sectarian Factions in Iraq: Sunni and Shi'ite

From the time of the fall of Baghdad during the 2003 U.S. invasion, sectarian violence increases in Iraq and threatens to deteriorate into civil war. A mixture of ethnic and religious tensions underlie the conflict even though the country is 95% Muslim (the remainder being Christian and Yezidi—adherents of Yazdanizm, a small ancient Middle Eastern religion largely composed of Iraqi Kurds). Of this population, approximately 60% is Shi'ite and 35% is Sunni, a reversal of the typical condition elsewhere in the Muslim world where Sunni Islam is the majority. Sunni and Shi'ite are the two main divisions of Islam, and though they both accept the major tenets of the tradition, they differ in their view of proper leadership of the community. The Sunni majority accepts the first four Caliphs (who are elected) as the legitimate successors of Muhammad, whereas the Shi'ite minority holds that Muhammad's successors, known as imams, should be chosen from among the descendants of the fourth Caliph, Ali, Muhammad's son-in-law and male representative of his blood lineage. Ethnic affiliations further complicate religious allegiances—of the Iraqi Shi'ite majority, most are Arabs, while the Sunni minority is divided, largely, between Kurds and Arabs.

Photo Credits

Socrates: Réunion des Musées Nationaux/Art Resource, NY; **Detail of a Page from Genesis**: The Pierpont Morgan Library/Art Resource, NY; **Bust of Plato**: Scala/Art Resource, NY; **Bust of Mercury (believed to be Aristotle)**: Alinari/Art Resource, NY; **King Solomon Reading the Torah, French Miniature**: The Granger Collection, New York; **Buddhist Monks at Monastery**: © Tim Page/CORBIS; **Mencius**: The Granger Collection, New York; **Chuang-Tzu**: The Granger Collection, New York; **Map of Macedonian Empire**: The Granger Collection, New York; **Rama and Lakshmana Shooting Arrows at the Demon Ravana**: Victoria & Albert Museum, London/Art Resource, NY; **The Consummate Confucian Expression "The Eulogy of Nikuan"**: Werner Forman/Art Resource, NY; **Alexandria Library**: The Granger Collection, New York; **Torah-Finger**: Erich Lessing/Art Resource, NY; **Pilar of Ashoka**: Bridgeman-Giraudon/Art Resource, NY; **Prajnaparamita, Book Containing Mahayana**: Erich Lessing/

Art Resource, NY; **Qin Shi Huang, First Emperor of China**: HIP/Art Resource, NY; **The Ruins of Beit Zur, Israel**: Erich Lessing/Art Resource, NY; **Commentary on the Apocalypse, by Beatus of Liebana**: The Pierpont Morgan Library/Art Resource, NY; **Standing Bodhisattva**: Bildarchiv Preussicher Kulturbesitz/Art Resource, NY; **Man Practicing Yoga**: © Andy Whale/CORBIS; **Worshipping at the Shrine of the Great Diabutsu**: Library of Congress Prints and Photographs Division Washington, D.C. (LOC); **Head of Pompey**: Alinari/Art Resource, NY; **The City of Alexandria in Egypt**: Erich Lessing/Art Resource, NY; **Domenico di Michelino**: Scala/Art Resource, NY; **Entry into Jerusalem**: Scala/Art Resource, NY; **Emperor Augustus Offering to the Gods**: Erich Lessing/Art Resource, NY; **'An Arch Druid in His Judicial Habit'**: HIP/Art Resource, NY; St. Paul Preaching to the Jews: Giraudon/Art Resource, NY; **Boddhisattva Kuan-Yin**: Erich Lessing/Art Resource, NY; **The**

Victorious Army of Titus with the Spoils from Jerusalem: Alinari/Art Resource, NY; **Meeting Room (Ruins) at Qumran**: Erich Lessing/Art Resource, NY; **Saint Mark. Gospel of Cisoing Abbey**: Giraudon/Art Resource, NY; **Text Page of Gospel of Matthew**: The Pierpont Morgan Library/Art Resource, NY; **The Beginning of the Gospel of St. Luke**: Art Resource, NY; **St. John Writing the Apocalypse**: Giraudon/Art Resource, NY; **Crucifixion**: The Pierpont Morgan Library/Art Resource, NY; **Head of Christ**: Erich Lessing/Art Resource, NY; **Artifacts from the Cave of Letters, Where Refugees hid during Bar Kokhba's Revolt**: The Granger Collection, New York; **A Group of Scribes Copying the "Tao te king"**: Erich Lessing/Art Resource, NY; **Illustration of the Avatamsaka Sutra**: Reunion des Musees Nationaux/Art Resource, NY; **Sefirotic Tree of Life**: The Granger Collection, New York; **The Boddhisattva Manjusri**: Reunion des Musees Nationaux/Art Resource, NY;

Inscription of the Kushan Language: Giraudon/Art Resource, NY; **Antique Chinese Taoist Priest's Robe**: © Peter Hardholdt/CORBIS; **The Figure of a Chac-Mool**: Erich Lessing/Art Resource, NY; **Torah shield**: Erich Lessing/Art Resource, NY; **Illustrated Manichaen Folio**: Bildarchiv Preussischer Kulturbesitz/Art Resource, NY; **Cross of Constantine**: Scala/Art Resource, NY; **Donation of Constantine**: Scala/Art Resource, NY; **Holy Sepulcher**: The Granger Collection, NY; **Zoroastrian Site of Fire Worship During Sassanian Period**: SEF/Art Resource, NY; **Relief from the Obelisk of Emperor Theodosius**: Vanni/Art Resource, NY; **The Column of Pompey**: SEF/Art Resource, NY; **The Sacred Well Kalichoron**: Erich Lessing/Art Resource, NY; **St. Augustine**: Alinari/Regione Umbria/Art Resource, NY; **Durga Slaying the Demon Buffalo Mahisha**: Borremeo/Art Resource, NY; **Fragment of a Mosaic from the Synagogue of Maon**: Snark/Art Resource, NY; **St. Patrick**:

The Granger Collection, New York; **Praying to Ganesha**: Bildarchiv Preussischer Kulturbesitz/Art Resource NY; **Mendicant Friar**: Erich Lessing/Art Resource, NY; **Buddhist Monk**: Scala/Art Resource, NY; **Saint Jerome in his Study**: The Granger Collection, New York; **Pope Leo I and Attila**: The Granger Collection, New York; **The Triumph of Orthodoxy**: HIP/Art Resource, NY; **Kabbalistic Symbol**: The Granger Collection, New York; **Bodhidharma**: Erich Lessing/Art Resource, NY; **Amida Butsa, the Great Buddha**: Werner Forman/Art Resource, NY; **Loch Ness Monster**: The Granger Collection, New York; **Ascent of Muhammed to Heaven**: Art Resource, NY; **Talmudist**: Snark/Art Resource, NY; **Page from the Koran**: Bridgeman-Giraudon/Art Resource, NY; **Schematic View of Medina**: Werner Forman/Art Resource, NY; **Grotto of Meditation**: Erich Lessing/Art Resource, NY; **Cave of Buddhas at Hangzhou**: © Earl & Nazima Kowall/CORBIS; **Mohammed and the First Three Caliphs**: Bildarchiv

Preussischer Kulturbesitz/Art Resource, NY; **Caliph Omar I**: The Granger Collection, New York; **The Third Orthodox Khalif, Uthman**: Victoria & Albert Museum, London/Art Resource, NY; **Koran, 8th century**: The Granger Collection, New York; **Ali ibn Abi Talib**: SEF/Art Resource, NY; **Arch of the Maqsurah**: Scala/Art Resource, NY; **The Dome of the Rock**: Erich Lessing/Art Resource, NY; **Story of Mangal-asva of the King of Benares**: Borromeo/Art Resource, NY; **Amaterasu, Shinto Goddess of the Sun**: Victoria & Albert Museum, London/Art Resource, NY; **Yomei-mon gate of the Shinto Shrine**: Scala/Art Resource, NY; **Battle of Poitiers (Tours)**: Reunion des Musees Nationaux/Art Resource, NY; **Gold Dinar**: Bildarchiv Preussischer Kulturbesitz/Art Resource, NY; **Three Levels of the World**: Erich Lessing/Art Resource, NY; **Indian Mystic Padmasambhava**: Erich Lessing/Art Resource, NY; **Carpenters and Masons at Work**: Erich Lessing/Art Resource, NY; **Portrait of Zoroaster**:

© Kazuyosgu Nomachi/CORBIS; **Orandasen**: LOC; **Priests Dressed as Black Hat Dancers for the Sacred 'Cham Dance**: Werner Forman/Art Resource, NY; **Persian Version by Balami of Universal History by Tabari**: Public Domain; **Ganden Monastery**: © Kazuyoshi Nomachi/CORBIS; **Indonesia: Monument**: The Granger Collection, New York; **Buddhism: Diamond Sutra**: The Granger Collection, New York; **Ascension of the Prophet Mohammed**: Bildarchiv Preussischer Kulturbesitz/Art Resource, NY; **Kneeling Dervish**: Snark/Art Resource, NY; **Cherry Blossoms and Warbler**: Reunion des Musees Nationaux/Art Resource, NY; **Abuali Sino Avicenna**: Creative Commons Attribution 2.5; **A Statue in the Form of a Portrait of a Deified Teacher**: Werner Forman/Art Resource, NY; **Detail of a Bronze Statue of Confucius at Confucius Temple, Nanjing**: © Keren Su/CORBIS; **Bronze figure of Milarepa**: HIP/Art Resource, NY; **Crusades: Peter the Hermit/Pope

Urban II**: The Granger Collection, New York; **India: Mughal Art**: The Granger Collection, New York; **Zhu Xi**: Public Domain; **Moses Mainonide Mishne Torah**: Giraudon/Art Resource, NY; **Scivias**: Erich Lessing/Art Resource, NY; **Diabutsu**: Art Resource, NY; **Saladin**: Public Domain; **Mecca**: American Colony (Jerusalem), LOC; **Innocent III**: The Granger Collection, New York; **Averroes**: The Granger Collection, New York; **Delacroix: Crusades**: The Granger Collection, New York; **Saint Dominic**: The Granger Collection, New York; **Albigensian Crusade**: The Granger Collection, New York; **St. Francis of Assisi**: The Granger Collection, New York; **Crusades: Engraving**: The Granger Collection, New York; **Hsuan Tsang**: The Granger Collection, New York; **St. Thomas Aquinas**: The Granger Collection, New York; **Pope Gregory IX**: The Granger Collection, New York; **Japanese Painting of Zen Monk**: Art Resource, NY; **Kuniyoshi: Oban Print. Nichiren Calming the Storm**: The Granger Collection, New

York; **Kabbalistic Analysis of the Mind**: Image Select/Art Resource, NY; **Mevlana Djalal ad-Rin Rumi**: The Pierpont Morgan Library/Art Resource, NY; **Meister Eckhard:** The Granger Collection, New York; **A Tibetan Tangka**: Erich Lessing/Art Resource, NY; **John Wycliffe**: The Granger Collection, New York; **Fresco Painting in Potala, Tibet**: © Charles & Josette Lenars/CORBIS; **Jan Hus Being Executed as a Heretic**: Snark/Art Resource, NY; **Joan of Arc Arrives at the Castle of Chinon**: Erich Lessing/Art Resource, NY; **Dancing Dervishes**: The Granger Collection, New York; **Page from the Gurenberg Bible**: Bildarchiv Preussischer Kulturbesitz/Art Resource, NY; **Bust of Philosopher Marsilio Ficino**: Erich Lessing/Art Resource, NY; **Guru Nanak**: Victoria & Albert Museum, London/Art Resource, NY; **Medieval Torture Chamber**: Erich Lessing/Art Resource, NY; **Execution of an Arsonist Witch by Burning at Stake**: Foto Marburg/Art Resource, NY; **King Ferdinand II of Aragon**: Bildarchiv

Preussischer Kulturbesitz/Art Resource, NY; **Savonarola Rejecting the Honors of Pope Alexander VI**: Alinari/Art Resource, NY; **Wang Yang Ming**: Public Domain; **The Creation of Adam**: Erich Lessing/Art Resource, NY; **Engraving of Martin Luther**: Foto Marburg/Art Resource, NY; **Siege of Christian Fortress**: Giraudon/Art Resource, NY; **Conquest of Mexico by the Spaniards**: Bildarchiv Preussischer Kulturbesitz/Art Resource, NY; **Martin Luther at the Reichstag of Worms in 1521**: Foto/Art Resource, NY; **The Luther Bible**: Foto Marburg/Art Resource, NY; **Pourbus, Frans the Elder**: Alinari/Art Resource, NY; **Burning of the Anabaptists at the Stake**: Foto Marburg/Art Resource, NY; **Beginning of the Gospel of St. John**: HIP/Art Resource, NY; *The Virgin of Guadalupe* **by Miguel Cabrera**: © Christie's Images/CORBIS; **Atahualpa Being Put to Death by Order of Pizzaro**: Giraudon/Art Resource, NY; **Gold Medal of Henry VIII**: HIP/Art Resource, NY; **Menno Simons**: The Granger Collection, New

York; **John Calvin in his Study**: Snark/Art Resource, NY; **The Miracle of Saint Francis Xavier**: Erich Lessing/Art Resource, NY; **Galileo Galilei**: The Granger Collection, NY; **St. John of the Cross**: The Granger Collection, New York; **The Council of Trent**: Scala/Art Resource, New York;; **Panel from the Codex Fejervary-Mayer**: Werner Forman/Art Resource, NY; **John Knox (1512–1572)**; The Granger Collection, New York; **Akbar**: Giraudon/Art Resource, NY; **Thangka: Dalai Lama**: The Granger Collection, New York; **Hermetic figures**: Snark/Art Resource, NY; **Teresa of Avila**: The Granger Collection, New York; **The Departure of the Pilgrim Fathers, for America, A.D. 1620**: LOC; **Golden Temple of Amritsar**: Borromeo/Art Resource, NY; **King James I Bible, 1611**: The Granger Collection, New York; **Landing at Plymouth**: The New York Public Library/Art Resource, NY; **Taj Mahal, Main Entrance**: Vanni/Art Resource; **The Potala Palace, Former Residence of the Dalai**

Lama: © Bob Krist/CORBIS; **Pogroms**: Erich Lessing/Art Resource, NY; **George Fox Preaching the Quaker Gospel Under the Oak Trees of Flushing, New York**: The Granger Collection, New York; **Baruch Spinoza**: HIP/Art Resource, NY; **Aurangzeb at Prayer**: Art Resource, NY; **Basho**: The Granger Collection, New York; **Shabbetai Tzevi**: The Granger Collection, New York; **"Fidelity"**: Reunion des Musees Nationaux/Art Resource, NY; **Salem Witch Trial**: The Granger Collection, New York; **Amish Man Driving Buggy**: © Richard T. Nowitz/CORBIS; **Jonathan Edwards**: The Granger Collection, New York; **The Clare Cross**: The Granger Collection, New York; **Iraq—Sunni Muslim Gathered for the Traditional Friday Prayers at the Al Imam Al Aadham Mosque**: © Fotoreport Federico Gambarini/dpa/CORBIS; **Portrait of John Wesley**: The Philadelphia Museum of Art/Art Resource, NY; **Emanuel Swedenborg**: Giraudon/Art Resource, NY; **Kedushat Levi**: The Granger

Collection, New York; **Jacob Frank, Polish-Jewish Mystic**: The Granger Collection, New York; **Moses Mendelssohn**: Erich Lessing/Art Resource, NY; **Touro Synagogue**: The Granger Collection, New York; **Shakers Dance**: Giraudon/Art Resource, NY; **Battle in the Rue de Rohan**: Giraudon/Art Resource, NY; **Methodist Revival in USA 1839**: Public Domain; **The Rosetta Stone**: © Bettmann/CORBIS; **Friedrich Schleiermacher**: The Granger Collection, New York; *The Rapture of St. Joseph*: Reunion des Musees Nationaux/Art Resource, NY; **Charles Grandison Finney**: The Granger Collection: New York; **Unitarian Church**: © G. E. Kidder Smith/CORBIS; **Portrait of Joseph Smith**: National Portrait Gallery, Smithsonian Institution/Art Resource, NY; **Monument to Soren Kierkegaard**: Snark/Art Resource, NY; **Brigham Young**: National Portrait Gallery, Smithsonian Institution/Art Resource, NY; **Brass Cash Coin of the Taiping Rebellion**: HIP/Art Resource, NY;

Immaculate Conception with Six Saints: Erich Lessing/Art Resource, NY; **Baha'i Center in Delhi**: © Tibor Bognar/CORBIS; **William Booth**: The Granger Collection, New York; **Advertisement by Mary Baker Eddy**: The Granger Collection, New York; **Man Praying at Dazaifu Tenmangu Shinto Shrine**: © Tibor Bognar/CORBIS; **Pope Pius IX: Anno Domini 1846**: LOC; **Mme. Blavatsky**: LOC; **Sri. Gri. Ramakrishna**: LOC; **Ghost Dance of the Sioux Indians in North America**: LOC; **Parliament of the World's Religions**: © Franklin McMahon/CORBIS; **Rabindranath Tagore**: Sukumar Ray, public domain; **Portrait of Albert Schweitzer**: Arthur William Heintzelman, LOC; **Matrimandir Meditation Facility**: © Christophe Boisvieux/CORBIS; **Sigmund Freud**: HIP/Art Resource, NY; **Jerusalem, Israel**: Erich Lessing/Art Resource, NY; **"Henta-Koi" Magical Charm**: Werner Forman/Art Resource, NY; **Martin Buber**: HIP/Art Resource; **John T. Scopes**: LOC; **Ein Volk, ein Reich,**

ein Fuehrer: Bildarchiv Preussischer Kulturbesitz/Art Resource, NY; **Tomb of Josemaria Excriva de Balaguer**: © Vittoriano Rastelli/CORBIS; **J. Krishnamurti**: LOC.; **Mohandas Gandhi**: The Granger Collection, New York; **Comte de Saint-Germain**: The Granger Collection, New York; **Emperor Haile Selassie in Addis Ababa**: © dpa/CORBIS; **Surrender of Japan on the *Missouri***: © Bettmann/CORBIS; **Pistis Sophia**: The Granger Collection, New York; **Dietrich Bonhoeffer**: The Granger Collection, New York; **Lord Mountbatten Meets with Indian Parties**: © Bettmann/CORBIS; **First Day of Jewish State**: © David Rubinger/CORBIS; **Dead Sea Scrolls and Caves and Qumran Excavations of Essene Monastery**: LOC; **Thomas Merton in Monastery Library**: © Horace Bristol/CORBIS; **Sai Baba at Puttaparti Ashram**: © Christophe Boisvieux/CORBIS; **Detail of Buddha from a Buddhist Shrine in Colombo, Sri Lanka**: © Pierre Vauthey/CORBIS SYGMA; **Buddha Statues in Kobe**: © Gavin

Hellier/Robert Harding World Imagery/CORBIS; **Paul Tillich**: © Bettmann/CORBIS; **Scientology Headquarters in Los Angeles**: © Jerry Dabrowski/dpa/CORBIS; **Pierre Teilhard de Chardin**: The Granger Collection, New York; **The "Dalits" March in India**: © Antoine Serra/In Visu/CORBIS; **Maharishi Mahesh Yogi**: © Bettmann/CORBIS; **Dalai Lama and Mother**: © Bettmann/CORBIS; **Prime Minister Speaking to Huge Crowd**: © Bettmann/CORBIS; **Opening Ecumenical Council at St. Peter's Basilica**: © Mettmann/CORBIS; **Martin Luther King Jr. at Ebenezer Baptist Church**: © Flip Schilke/CORBIS; **Malcolm X Ives Press Conference**: © Bettmann/CORBIS; **Map Showing Israeli Gains from Six Day War**: © Bettmann/CORBIS; **South Korean Evangelist Reverend Moon Sun-Myung Blesses Newlyweds in Seoul**: © Reuters/CORBIS; **Bengalis Cheer Indian Troops in Dacca**: © Bettmann/CORBIS; **Rabbi Blessing Wine**: © Bettmann/CORBIS; **Borobudur Temple**: © Free Agents

Limited/ CORBIS; **Makeshift Memorial to Cambodian Victims of Pol Pot**: © Doug Niven/epa/CORBIS; **Episcopalian Bishop Barbara Harris**: © Reuters/CORBIS; **Pope John Paul II in Strasbourg**: © Thierry Orban/CORBIS SYGMA; **Iranian Revolution—Ayatollah Khomeini**: © Patrick Chauvel/SYGMA/CORBIS; **"Rajneesh" Community in Oregon**: © JP Laffont/SYGMA/CORBIS; **Archbishop Desmond Tutu Hands over Final Report to the South African President Thabo Mbeki**: © Reuters/CORBIS; **Detail of *Deesis* Mosaic in Hagia Sophia**: © Hanan Isachar/CORBIS; **The Dalai Lama. Laureate of the Nobel Peace Prize**: © Pelletier Micheline/CORBIS SYGMA; **Girl Carrying Sign Vowing to Kill Salman Rushdie**: © Reuters/CORBIS; **Aung San Suu Kyi**: © Emmanuel Dunand/epa/CORBIS; **Babri Mosque**: © Hulton-Deutsch Collection/CORBIS; **Explosion at Branch Davidian Compound**: © Greg Smith/CORBIS; **Taliban Fighters Pose with Their Weapons in Kandahar**: ©

Reuters/CORBIS; **Crowd Gathers for the Million Man March**: © Jacques M. Chenet/CORBIS; **Aum Shinrikyo Guru Asahara Shoko**: © Sankei Shimbun/CORBIS SYGMA; **Bill Graham**: Warren K. Leffler, LOC; **Mother Teresa** © Reuters/CORBIS; **Video of Marchall Herff Applewhite**: © Brooks Kraft/CORBIS; **Portrait of Author Salman Rushdie**: © Christopher J. Morris/CORBIS; **Reverend Jerry Falwell with Bible**: © William Coupon/CORBIS; **Chinese Plainclothes Policeman Stands Guard on Beijing's Tiananmen Gate**: © Reuters/CORBIS; **The ABC Television Network 2004 Summer Press Tour All-Star Party**: © Frank Trapper/CORBIS; **Hazara Fighters Squat with Their Kalashnikovs Near Where a Giant Buddha Statue once Stood in Bamiyan**: © Reuters/CORBIS; **Firefighters at World Trade Center**: © Neville Elder/CORBIS; **Cardinal Bernard Francis Law**: © Grzegorz Galazka/CORBIS; **Iranian Lawyer Ebadi Poses with Nobel Diploma after Receiving Nobel**

Peace Prize: © Scanpix/Tor Richardsen/Pool/Reuters/CORBIS; **Robinson Consecrated as First Openly Gay Bishop**: © Dan Habib/Concord Monitor/CORBIS; **Movie Marquee Shows Sold Out**: © Jeff Mitchell/Reuters/CORBIS; **Buddhist Monk Party of Sri Lanka**: © M. A. Pushpa Mumara/epa/CORBIS; **Pope John Paul II's Funeral in St. Peter's Square**: © Alessandra Benedetti/CORBIS; **Pope Benedict XVI**: © Alessandra Benedetti/CORBIS

Index

The Illustrated Timeline of
Art History

The Illustrated Timeline of
Science

The Illustrated Timeline of
The Universe